Great Games

for 4th–6th Graders

Zondervan/Youth Specialties Books

Amazing Tension Getters
Called to Care
Creative Socials and Special Events
Get 'Em Talking
Good Clean Fun
Good Clean Fun, Volume 2
Great Games for 4th–6th Graders (Get 'Em Growing)
Great Ideas for Small Youth Groups
Greatest Skits on Earth
Greatest Skits on Earth, Volume 2
Growing Up in America
High School Ministry
High School TalkSheets
Holiday Ideas for Youth Groups (Revised Edition)
Hot Talks
Ideas for Social Action
Intensive Care: Helping Teenagers in Crisis
Junior High Ministry
Junior High TalkSheets
The Ministry of Nurture
On-Site: 40 On-Location Programs for Youth Groups
Organizing Your Youth Ministry
Play It! Great Games for Groups
Teaching the Truth about Sex
Tension Getters
Tension Getters II
Unsung Heroes: How to Recruit and Train Volunteer Youth Workers
Up Close and Personal: How to Build Community in Your Youth Group
Youth Specialties Clip Art Book
Youth Specialties Clip Art Book, Volume 2

Great Games

for 4th–6th Graders

DAVID LYNN

Zondervan Publishing House
Grand Rapids, Michigan

Disclaimer

This book (like life) contains games that, in an unfortunate combination of circumstances, could result in emotional or physical harm. You'll need to evaluate each game on its own merit for your group, for each game's potential risk, for safety precautions that must be taken, advance preparation that must be required, and possible results before you use a game. Youth Specialties, Inc., is not responsible—nor has it any control over—the use or misuse of any of the games published in this book.

Great Games for 4th-6th Graders

Copyright © 1990 by Youth Specialties, Inc.

Youth Specialties Books, 1224 Greenfield Drive, El Cajon, California 92021,
are published by Zondervan Publishing House,
1415 Lake Drive, S.E., Grand Rapids, Michigan 49506

Library of Congress Cataloging in Publication Data

Lynn, David, 1954–
    Great games for 4th–6th graders : get 'em growing / by David Lynn.
        p.   cm.
    ISBN 0-310-52541-1
    1. Games—United States. 2. Group games. I. Title II. Title: Great games for fourth-sixth graders.
GV1204.12.L96 1990
793'.0973—dc20   90-33482
                                                                  CIP

All Scripture quotations, unless otherwise noted, are taken from the *Holy Bible: New International Version* (North American Edition). Copyright © 1973, 1978, 1984 by the International Bible Society. Used by permission of Zondervan Bible Publishers.

Edited by J. Cheri McLaughlin
Designed by Jack Rogers
Illustrations by Dan Pegoda
Typeset by Leah Perry

Printed in the United States of America

90 91 92 93 94 95 96 97 98 99 / EB / 10 9 8 7 6 5 4 3 2 1

ABOUT THE *YouthSource*™ PUBLISHING GROUP

YOUTHSOURCE books, tapes, videos, and other resources pool the expertise of three of the finest youth-ministry resource providers in the world:

Campus Life Books—the publishers of the award-winning *Campus Life* magazine, who for nearly fifty years have helped high schoolers live a Christian life.

Youth Specialties—serving ministers to middle-school, junior-high, and high-school youth for over twenty years through books, magazines, and training events such as the National Youth Workers Convention.

Zondervan Publishing House—one of the oldest, largest, and most respected evangelical Christian publishers in the world.

Campus Life
465 Gundersen Drive
Carol Stream, IL 60188
708/260-6200

Youth Specialties
1224 Greenfield Drive
El Cajon, CA 92021
619/440-2333

Zondervan
1415 Lake Drive S.E.
Grand Rapids, MI 49506
616/698-6900

To my foster kids
Jeanine, Michelle, and Paul

Table of Contents

A recent drive through my old home neighborhood brought back childhood memories—endless hours of playing kick the can, breaking a neighbor's window during a pick-up game of baseball, playing leapfrog, doing cakewalks at the PTA carnival. Passing by my old elementary school, now boarded up, I flashed on spit-wad fights, tetherball championships, dodge-ball wars, and playing kickball during recess. I remembered making up rules as we played and avoiding the house of the neighborhood grouch.

Play is changing for today's children, however. Youth sports organizations, the fastest growing organizations in youth work, have made games more organized, more professionalized, more competitive. Elementary schools paint the hopscotch squares on playground sidewalks, eliminating the need for children to scratch out their own outline with a rock. After-school programs have paid child-care specialists ready with organized sporting events. What was fun for me and you has become work for the children of the 1990s.

What might you hear on the playgrounds and playing fields in America today? Dennis Maloney, a veteran youth worker, made this observation:

> Listen to hear if the laughter has been replaced with a stern silence. Watch the faces of the participants to see if the look of excitement now borders on a look of fear. Feel to sense if the opposing teams' attitude toward one another have shifted from a friendly respect to an intense opposition. Finally, try to determine whether the element of fun still fills the air. If you visited many of the playgrounds I have been to, you would sense that the environment of children's sports has changed drastically and that, with few exceptions, the games children once played have now become the toils of children. (From "Coaching Our Kids," in *New Designs for Youth Development*, January-February 1982.)

The competitive nature of American play has stressed our children out. Its intense, competitive spirit has spilled over into the Boy Scout troop meeting, the 4-H demonstration, and of course, the classroom. Elementary-school teachers readily tell horror stories of tense, stressed kids.

"What's wrong with a little competition?" you ask. "It's the real world!" The real world for adults, maybe—but for children? Our preoccupation with winning has made losers out of both children and adults, for we have forgotten how to play for the fun of it. It's almost uncool for older children and adolescents to have fun playing games. Young people are looking for a way to have fun—and partying with drugs and alcohol is a socially acceptable way to play.

Keep this in mind as you plan games: Fun for fun's sake is okay. There's a place in children's ministry for fun. After all, Christ's first miracle was at a party. So take this book and go have some fun! And remember, you don't have to keep score.

Acknowledgements

Great Games for Kids includes a varied collection of games suitable for the upper elementary grades. You may recognize many of the games as those you played in grade school—some of which are still popular with today's kids. Some traditional games have a new twist, while others are completely new. Many of the games originally appeared in the *Ideas* Library, published by Youth Specialties, Inc.

I would like to thank all of the creative people responsible for developing and testing the games found in this book. Without their dedication to young people, *Great Games for Kids* would not have been possible.

David Lynn

Play Directions

Fourth, fifth, and sixth grades—these upper elementary years lay the groundwork for a child's self-image and identity that affects the rest of the child's life. Developmental psychologist Eric Erikson long ago discovered that experiences in elementary school gave a child either a sense of competence or feelings of inferiority and helplessness. It is during the elementary school years that young people hopefully develop the skills and abilities that enhance their self-worth and help them make a healthy transition into adolescence and adulthood. Children unable to attain a healthy sense of competence develop instead a basic sense of worthlessness, inadequacy, and inferiority, making it more difficult for them to move healthily through the adolescent years.

Before attending school, a child's sense of identity is derived largely from the family. During the elementary school years, however, the influence of the school, church, neighborhood, child-care industry, and media grows significantly. All of these institutions and people provide children with feedback about who they are. Children evaluate themselves and their competence by comparing their looks, skills, and abilities with schoolmates, TV children, Sunday-school-paper children, and neighbors. As a children's worker you are concerned about how children feel about themselves because you know how profoundly self-image impacts their lives. Play, believe it or not, has tremendous potential to affect a child's sense of self.

Play gives children the chance to both learn and test out their competencies by showing off new-found motor skills, by exercising their imaginations and sparking their creativity, and by offering them experience in collaborating with peers and adults to achieve a common goal. When young people play a game like Time-Warp Tag (page 42), they feel a sense of achievement because they were able to successfully participate. Play helps kids assert their competence and self-worth.

But play can also have unintended negative consequences. If young people are placed in situations where only the brightest and the best achieve, what will they learn about themselves? Remember that children evaluate their sense of self and their feelings of worth by comparing their achievements to the achievements of others. Play, whether informal games or formalized sporting events, can easily create in children feelings of insecurity about their competence. Since children do not possess adult coping skills, they have a difficult time separating individual experiences from a general evaluation of their personal worth. They can only handle being picked last for a team so many times before they begin believing that they really are inferior.

Arrange games to contribute to every child a sense of competence rather than creating insecurity. Catering our play experiences to the popular kids, allowing put-downs, or focusing on winning and losing have no place in children's work. Children created in God's image are fragile. We must handle them with care and provide them with play experiences that they can look back upon fondly.

Teaching Kids (and Adults) How To Play

"It's not whether you win or lose, it's how you play the game"—or so we've heard. But somewhere along the way, "how you play the game" was lost. Yet how the game is played is why games need to be played. Recapturing this attitude of play is difficult. The following tips can help you restore a playful attitude within your group.

Be patient with children (and adults) who do not know how to have fun playing a game. Being cool requires a certain aloofness that prohibits some from having fun. Others are so preoccupied with winning that they lose the joy of play. Your group may not readily embrace a new philosophy of play. Be willing to give them time and many play experiences in order to lose the cool or jock image.

Young people learn more from watching you than from listening to you. A new attitude towards fun and games will more likely be caught than taught. That means you must start with changing the way adults in your group view games. If your adult leaders sit on the sidelines while expecting the kids to play, then your young people will likely opt out of playing at any excuse. If your adults push the kids to win, your games will be tense and competitive. If, however, adults who work with children jump into the fun, their excitement will be contagious. When the adults stand along the sidelines, grab their hands and pull them into play. And when they go overboard with competition, gently remind them the purpose of play is not winning but celebrating by playing.

Competition is not bad; it's the kind *of competition that you need to monitor.* The most appropriate games involve unskilled competition—competition that requires skills that challenge all the players, not just the athletic types. Choose games that require dexterity as well as raw speed, thinking as well as reacting, subjective as well as objective responses. Games that give all the players an equal chance at winning allow everyone to have fun, not just the winners. You know you have healthy competition when the kids forget about keeping score. Structure games to equalize the competition, giving all players an equal chance to participate and succeed. At this age in particular, this is vital!

Choose games for this age group that build self-esteem. Avoid ending a game with a traditional winner (the one on top) and losers (those at the bottom). Structure the winning and losing around team efforts and present the whole team with any awards. Team winning makes it easier for the whole group to feel good about playing. (Be sure the award can be shared by all the team.) As your group experiences games that teach this new attitude of playing for fun, they will apply it when playing games that are traditionally competitive as well. Even the jock types can learn to want everyone to succeed and to play for the sheer enjoyment of play.

Explain games clearly and quickly. When introducing a game to your group, you first must have everyone's attention. This can be done by first extending an invitation for everyone to play. Give people a choice. Then use the following tips to get the game started:

- Assure players, through your gestures and tone of voice, that the game will be fun and will build them up.
- Explain and demonstrate the game in a way that all the players can hear you and see your face. Confusion during the game's explanation will frustrate kids before you even start playing.
- Tell the kids the name of the game, explain step-by-step how to play, and then demonstrate the game with another player or players.
- Show your excitement about playing the game—be a little wild and crazy. If

playing the game is fun, why not make the presentation of the game fun as well? Your play attitude is contagious. Use the KISMIF principle: Keep it simple; make it fun.

- Lead the kids in a practice round of the game. This reassures the group that you want to focus on having fun rather than winning/losing. A trial run also builds trust in the play process and in the group.
- Don't take the game so seriously that you get angry with players for not getting the rules. Let your irritation signal you to move on to another game or activity.
- If the game you are explaining requires teams, divide the group before you explain the rules. If the game requires a circle, circle up before presenting the game. This makes it easier to move from the explanation to the demonstration to the practice round and finally into the game itself.

Choosing the Right Game

Young people in grades four, five, and six are growing in their skills and abilities. As their speed and endurance increases, they become more accurate in throwing, kicking, dodging, stopping, and starting, and their interest in team competition intensifies. Simply because kids are interested in playing games, however, don't assume that any game will do. Consider the following factors when you select a game from this or any game book.

Decide upon a purpose. Obviously, we lead kids in games so that players can have fun. While this is important, there are other reasons for playing games as well. Perhaps you want to become better acquainted, burn off energy, practice cooperation, or teach a truth. Playing games can achieve all of these purposes—but you need to know your aim before you can select an appropriate game. And remember, it's okay to play games simply for their enjoyment (Prov. 17:22).

Include all players. Don't let the personality trap dictate your choice of games. Leaders often choose games that the popular, sharp-looking, jock-type kids like. These personality kids become the litmus test for a game's success or failure. Game leaders who cater to the beautiful kids when selecting games neglect the needs of the other kids that make up a group. Give each of your kids opportunities to be "It," to select a favorite game, or to participate as a safety guard. Take a risk and venture into unplayed territory; don't just play the popular favorites.

Involve the players in the choice. Young people in partnership with adults need to make play decisions. This does not mean that adult leaders abdicate their responsibilities in favor of kids making all the decisions. Rather, it's young people and adults choosing together the kinds of games they want to play.

Prepare for play. Some games require the leader to prepare game props or to adjust the play area before explaining the game. Some games require the players to come prepared—to wear grubbies, for example, for Tire Bowling (page 102), since the tires leave dirt and black marks on clothing. Choose games for which you and the players are adequately prepared, but don't neglect games that require a little preparation work. The extra time and effort is usu-ally rewarded with great fun.

Be sensitive to the co-ed question. For some games it's best to separate the boys from the girls. Generally, the more physical the game, the more likely that the girls should play the game separately from the boys. Although boys are not necessarily tougher and girls more fragile, kids in this age group are at different stages of development and won't always be comfortable playing co-ed. Games like Expandable Hopscotch (page 104), for instance, may suit girls but bore boys.

Consider group size. Some games like Crockball (page 91) can be played by large groups of young people, while others like Soccer on Paper (page 100) are best played with smaller groups of players. Still others like Shark in the Water (page 40) can be played equally as well and with as much fun in either a small or large group of players. If you have too many players for a game, break your group into smaller groups or modify how the game is played. For example, playing Soccer on Paper is just as much fun when players rotate in.

Adjust games for the physically challenged. Mentally retarded, handicapped, and other physically-challenged young people need to be included as much as possible in the group's fun. Imagination and prayer can turn up creative ways to involve all kids. If you're playing one of the Wacky Sports Events (see Chapters Eight and Nine) that requires kicking a ball, team up the child confined to a wheelchair, for instance, with a child who can run. Allow the child in the wheelchair to throw or bat the ball while the other child runs the pattern. A blind child can be the one that players tag in a relay event. When making modifications to accommodate the physically challenged, however, think safety first!

Go easy on food games. I believe that games requiring food should not be played unless the food is going to be eaten. Playing with eggs that will most likely be broken and thrown away gives young people the wrong message in a world where many people would gladly eat what the game players are sweeping up for the garbage can.

You are the final authority. Since you know your group of young people better than others, it is ultimately up to you to decide which games will be the best for your group. Just because a game is printed in a book does not mean it is suitable or safe *for your group of players.* Please use only the game ideas that best fit your group's personality, locale, size, playing space, and age. Don't be afraid to try something new once in a while, but don't feel you *have* to use a game just because it is in a book.

Choosing Your Play Area

A suitable place for play is as important as the right games. The most important consideration is, of course, safety. Use common sense when selecting a play area. Clear outdoor play areas of rocks, sticks, glass, and other potentially dangerous objects and debris. If the area is suitable except for a little pothole or two, cover them with a Frisbee and point them out to the group. Large holes, protruding sprinkler heads, trees, or other permanent, hazardous objects mean you must find a different play area.

Keep an indoor play area away from windows, stairways, and furniture. Clear the area of dangerous objects or obstacles. Choose only those games that

can be safely played in an area the size of yours. Some games designed for large, outdoor spaces just aren't fun to play in a confined area.

Safety First (and Second and Third)

Thinking about safety is a must for every game leader. Common sense will help you select a game, choose equipment, decide on a place to play, line up adult supervision, and actually play the game. A good rule of thumb: If it doesn't feel safe, assume it's not safe and don't play!

Vitally important to safely playing any game are the *safety guards*. A safety guard is a referee plus. Some safety guards referee the games, some lead the games, and others participate in play. Safety guards are given ultimate authority when it comes to running a game. If they see play getting out of hand, they can call a time-out. If a player is participating irresponsibly, a safety guard can talk one on one with that player about safety. Safety guards need to be prepared for their role; asking them to read this chapter is a good start.

Although safety guards are usually adults, kids can also act as safety guards. Designate a different young person as a safety guard for each game you play. Rotating the responsibility around the group helps your kids recognize their personal responsibility for safety. Players will take safety more seriously if they have been in the role of safety guard.

Insure the safety of your players and leaders by first playing the game yourself or at least watching as it's played. If you cannot either watch it or play it, get a group of your safety guards together and play the game. This helps you to know what to look for while playing the game with your kids. If you have never played Mad Hatter (page 60), for example, then you don't know that some kids are tempted to forget about the hats and just womp on other players. It's crucial to preview the game to look at as many safety angles as possible. Then when you teach the kids how to play it, you can include safety cautions with your directions.

The following safety checks can help you and your safety guards create a safe and fun playing experience.

- *Boundary check.* Clearly mark boundaries of play and point out the boundaries to the players. If you have not clearly pointed out and marked the playing area when playing Blind Man's Buff (page 32), for example, the blindfolded player could easily bump into something that may cause an injury.
- *Hazards check.* Remove debris and repair or mark other hazards in the playing area. Players need to remove watches, jewelry, pencils, or anything else they are wearing with which they could hurt themselves or others during play.
- *Rules check.* State the object of the game and explain its rules step-by-step. Play a practice round to observe if all the players know how to play. Too often players will nod their heads, indicating they understand the rules without really comprehending them. Play more than one practice round, if necessary. Players entering the game should first be checked out by a safety guard.
- *Break check.* All players should be allowed a personal time-out any time during play. It is imperative that players feel physically and psychologi-

cally safe while playing. Players out of breath or feeling threatened by a game need the option to walk away from play. At any time during the game a player can yell, "Break time. Stop!" and play will immediately stop. This offers an immediate out to injured or exhausted players. Explain the time-out and break-time rules before each play event occurs.

- *Safety guard check.* Are there enough safety guards for this game to be safe? Have the safety guards been prepared for their roles? These are two questions the game leader must ask himself before play. (By the way, don't play without safety guards just because a game in this book does not mention using them.)

Creating Play

Play does not just happen—it is created. Game leaders must create an environment where an attitude of play can flourish.

Consider that players are number one. Players are the reasons you are playing. Don't allow a game to own the players. Empower players with the attitude and skills to own a game. Once I was going to play Hot Towel (page 49) with a group of young people, but we had no towel. One of the players pulled out a foam ball and suggested we use it instead. We did! That's one way players own the game. Flexibility is the key. Don't feel locked into strict adherence to a prescribed way of playing a game.

Involve Adults. Young people need to see adults having fun. All too often young people play games with an adult leader while the rest of the adult workers talk to each other on the sidelines.

Plan for the unexpected. Weather, group mood, and attendance are only three of the myriad surprises for a game leader. If you are planning an outdoor event, prepare a few backup indoor games in case of rain, sleet, hail, or gloom of night. As unpredictable as the weather is the mood and interest of your group. What works with your kids one month may not work the next. Plan extra games to spark their interest if things begin to slow down. Be ready for a smaller or larger group than you expected. Either bring a backup set of games for both large and small groups, or be prepared to modify the games you have chosen.

Timing is everything. Let the energy level and fun level of your kids determine how long to play a game. End a game while players are still having fun. If you keep playing until they lose interest, they will remember the boredom rather than the fun of the game. But don't end games so soon that kids feel they didn't have a chance to have fun. Use time to add excitement or lift tension in a game. In some games shortening the time limit hypes kids to play wholeheartedly. If you notice kids looking overwhelmed or frustrated, however, give them more time to do their action.

There are no such things as official rules. The only rules that should be strictly enforced are the ones that affect safety. Young people in the fourth, fifth, and sixth grades are learning the flexibility and relativity of rules, a skill foundational to more complex learning. Giving children the opportunity to change the rules or create new rules is healthy. At this age one child will say, "Last one to the house is it," and a second child

retorts with, "Not included!" The first child then yells back, "No say-backs." This is an example of children using their new-found ability to manipulate rules—all part of normal, healthy development.

Changing the rules or creating new ones is also a great way to energize a game. By modifying rules players are actually creating a new game. Point out to players that when they change rules and modify games they are taking charge of creating their own play. To keep the playing happy, though, rule changes need to be agreed upon as a group before play begins.

A New Attitude Toward Winning and Losing

Many games have winners and losers, and in most games some players will do better than others. But as a game leader, you can help redefine and refocus the win/lose concept by leading your kids to evaluate their game times, by choosing team games, by using untraditional scoring methods, by choosing games that include non-athletic skills, and by making your safety guards your partners in changing old attitudes of competition.

Take advantage of teachable moments that sometimes follow play events to process what happened during the games. Discuss with the group what they learned from the play experience and how they felt about the competition. Lead them to remember the times during the games when certain players did their best—even if those players did not end up winning. By verbally recognizing non-winners who either improved or tried their hardest, you help kids learn to enjoy personal stretching rather than proving they are better than everyone else. (Don't try to evaluate every play experience, however.)

Another way to redefine winning and losing is by emphasizing team rather than individual competition. Team winning is different than individual victory because it requires cooperation among the team members to win. And the team that does not win does so as a team, avoiding the focus on one player either winning or not winning. When you discuss with the kids their views on competition, avoid using the word *loser*.

Scoring is another means of refocusing the win/lose concept. Traditionally scoring has had the effect of focusing play on the outcome; who wins and who loses. When this is the case with a group of kids, discontinue keeping score. You can create a new challenge and a whole new spirit to game playing by changing the way you score. Begin to give points for things players wouldn't expect. Traditionally points are awarded for the swiftest and the most, but you can give points for the funniest, the most creative, or for cooperation. For example, if you are playing Bubble-Blow Blitz (page 80), you can give points for the biggest bubbles instead of the most bubbles. Doing this also generates new enthusiasm for playing the game, especially when a game begins to slow. Make sure you include the players when you want to create a new scoring system. Train your players to look for new ways to score the games you play.

Random Scores

Next time your group is having competition between teams in several events and you want to "neutralize" things so

that no team is able to dominate the other teams, here's a way to hand out points that narrows the gap. Before the competition begins, determine the point value for each event. Make sure you have enough points so that every team will receive points following every event. (For example, if you have five teams, you need at least five point entries—10, 8, 6, 4, 2) Make up a board for each event like the illustration below, and scramble the points so that they are in no particular order.

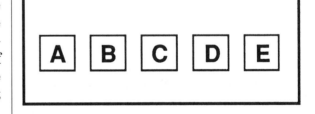

Then cover the points with construction paper squares with a letter on each one, like so:

| A | B | C | D | E |

Following every event, the points are awarded this way: The team that comes in first gets *first choice* of the letters on the board. They receive the number of points written underneath the letter they chose. Their score is purely chance, but they do get to choose first. The second place team chooses second, and so on. Sometimes the last place team actually gets the most points because no one knows how many points lie behind each letter. The first place team is generally satisfied with the privilege of choosing first, even though in the end the scores are determined by luck. Not only does this keep the competition close, but watching teams choose their letters adds extra suspense. Remember, you will need to make up a different board for each event.

Scoring can also be changed by giving away 10 points or 100 points to the placing teams or individuals. Kids will want to play their best when they can get 100 or 1000 points (who wants to play for one point?). Keep the spread between points small so that the last place team or person is still fairly close to the first place. For example, with three teams, first place may be 500 points, second place 475, and third place 450. That way the team in last still gets lots of points

and has achieved something.

Also remember unskilled competition when trying to create a new attitude toward winners and losers. If kids know they can compete successfully because different kinds of skills are required, they'll not only be more eager to play but their idea of who is a winner changes.

Finally, safety guards can help you redefine the win/lose attitude. Train your safety guards to referee events in such a way that competition is equalized. They can do this by focusing more intently on infractions of the winning teams or individuals and go easier on whoever is behind. The players will soon realize that the safety guards are always taking the side of the underdog. After a while players will focus more on having fun rather than earning points or keeping score.

Choosing "It"/
Choosing Teams

This chapter is dedicated to all those adults who experienced the humiliation of being picked last on a team as a kid. Use these creative games to make a fun and positive game out of a usually tough task.

Birthday "It"

Ask someone in the group of players to call out a month of the year. The player whose birthday falls closest to the first day of the called month is "It." If March was called out, for example, ask all the players born in March to raise their hands. Then ask who was born closest to March first—that player begins the game as "It."

Coin Toss "It"

If your group has outgrown rhymes and is searching for a more mature way to pick "It," try the following method. Select a player to call heads or tails as you flip a coin. If the player is correct, she takes the coin, goes to another player, and flips the coin while the other player calls heads or tails. If the call is incorrect, the player that flipped the coin is eliminated from beginning the game as "It," and the leader goes to another player. This continues until only one player is left, and that player becomes "It." This method works best with small groups.

One Potato, Two Potato

If your group is still willing to use a rhyme to choose "It," here's how to use rhymes. The kids stand in a circle or a line with one of their hands held in front of them, palm up. For every word or phrase of the rhyme, the leader slaps one of the players' hands. The person whose hand the leader slaps as she says the last word or phrase of the rhyme is eliminated from beginning the game as "It." The leader continues rhyming and slapping hands until all but one of the players are eliminated. That player begins the game as "It."

Remember this chant for choosing who was to play "It" first?

Eeny meeny miney moe,
Catch a rabbit by the toe.
If he hollers, let him go.
My mother says to pick this one

right over here.

For a creative twist, recite an old rhyme like Eeny Meeny Miney Moe to the group and ask them to come up with their own contemporary version. Or use the following long-lived rhyme (many of your players may know it already):

One potato, two potatoes,
Three potatoes, four.
Five potatoes, six potatoes,
Seven potatoes, more.

In this example the leader would say, "One potato" while slapping the hand of a player, "Two potatoes" while slapping the next player's hand, and so on. Each time the leader gets to the word "more," the player whose hand is slapped is eliminated from being "It." The last player left becomes "It."

Rock, Paper, Scissors

This classic game can be used to pick "It." Ask all the players to form a circle facing outward. The players can make three hand symbols: a rock (represented by a clenched fist), paper (a flat, open hand), or scissors (two fingers opened like the blades of scissors). A rock "breaks" scissors, paper "covers" rock, and scissors "cut" paper. When the leader signals "One, two, three, go!" everyone turns around to face the inside of the circle with one outstretched hand representing either a rock, paper, or scissors. Players who are beaten must sit down. Players left standing turn around, the leader repeats the count, and the players face back inside the circle displaying one of the three symbols. The last player left standing begins the game as "It."

Balloon Bust

This is a good way to choose couples for a game needing pairs. Give half the group pieces of paper on which to write their names. Tell them to put the paper with their name on it inside balloons, one paper per balloon. Ask them to blow up the balloons and tie them. Mix all the balloons up in the middle of the room. On a signal each person in the half of the group whose names are not in the balloons grabs a balloon, pops it, reads the name on the paper inside, and pairs with the person whose name was in the balloon.

Domino Teams

Make up 4 x 6 cards to look like dominoes. Create as many sets as you plan to have teams, each set in a different color. In each set make a run of numbers that equals the number of players you plan to have on each team (i.e., four teams of seven people would have sets of cards in red, blue, green, and black, with each set having cards of one dot through seven respectively). Tape one card on the back of each player.

When all the dominoes are used, explain to the group that at the whistle they are to discover the color and number of the dominos they are wearing. They may ask only questions that other players can answer with a "yes" or a "no." A player can ask a particular person only one question. When all have found out the colors and numbers of their dominoes, they go to their team areas (areas should be designated prior to starting the choosing game). Eventually all the teams will be in the right areas, and everyone will have had fun and gotten better acquainted in the process.

Gather By . . .

One of the worst methods of choosing teams is to select two captains who take turns picking their favorites. How about trying this one for a change of pace? Ask the players to gather into groups based upon certain characteristics like the following:

- Gather by the school you attend. (If too many schools are represented, combine schools together to form more equal teams.)
- Gather by birthday. All players born on odd-numbered days on one team, and all players born on even-numbered days on the other team.
- Gather by the first letter of the players' last names. Names beginning with A–L make up one team, names beginning with M–Z make up the second team. (If you need more teams, break up the alphabet accordingly.)
- Gather by birth-month. (Combine months to form the number of teams you need.)
- Gather by hair color.
- Gather by eye color.
- Gather by color of socks.
- Gather by flavor of bubble gum. (Distribute sticks of flavored gum just before you begin, equal numbers of one flavor for each team you need.)

When teams are not equal, the leader can select several players to move to other teams to make them even.

Painters' Caps

Have you tried every possible way to distinguish teams from each other—headbands, arm bands, balloons tied to wrists, etc., etc.? Try dyed painters' caps—you can keep them from event to event or give them to the kids as mementos.

Most paint stores carry inexpensive, cloth painters' caps. Soak them in dye (the Rit brand works well) for ten to fifteen minutes, then tumble dry each color separately. The brighter the colors, the easier to tell teams apart. Hand them out to kids as they arrive, and when all your players are ready to play, teams are already selected.

Rock, Paper, Scissors Revisited

One of the oldest, simplest, and easiest methods for deciding which team goes first is the coin toss. But if your group is looking for a fresh approach, try Rock, Paper, Scissors (page 26). Ask the teams to huddle to choose their hand signal. Then line up the two teams facing each other and blow the whistle. The unbeaten team gets to go first.

Shuffle the Deck

Here's a simple, lively way to break a large group into teams. Distribute a deck of playing cards to the group, one card per player. Then call out different combinations, such as
• "Get in a group that adds up to fifty-eight."
• "Find three people of the same suit."

• "Find five numbers in a row of any suit."
• "Find your whole suit."
• "Find four of you—four 3s, four 8s, etc."
For larger groups use multiple decks of cards; for smaller groups eliminate cards. Then you can create your own combinations!

CHAPTER 3

Touch 'n' Tag Games

The toughest thing about tag can be deciding who will begin as "It." Once tag games begin, though, who knows when they will end.

This game requires four teams of equal size. Each team takes one corner of the room or playing field. The play area can be either square or rectangular. On a signal (e.g., whistle) each team attempts to move as quickly as possible to the corner diagonally across from their corner, performing an announced activity as they go. The first team to get all its members into its new corner wins that particular round. The first round can be simply running to the opposite corner, but after that you can use any number of possibilities: walking backward, wheelbarrow racing (one person is the wheelbarrow), piggyback, rolling somersaults, hopping on one foot, skipping, crab walking, etc. There will be literally mass bedlam in the center as all four teams crisscross. Alert your safety guards to referee the confusion in the middle where the lines cross.

Blind Man's Buff

This game is mistakenly called Blind Man's Bluff rather than Buff (the word buff is an old English word for buffet). Here is one of several popular variations of this classic tag game.

The player chosen to be "It" is blindfolded, spun around three times in the middle of the circle of players, and turned loose to hunt for another player. "Its" objective is to grab hold of another player and guess the player's name (captured players cannot struggle). If "It" can guess the identity of the captured player, that player becomes the new "It." However, if "It" cannot guess correctly, he remains "It" for another round. The other players are confined to a boundaried, safe playing area that is patrolled by safety guards. While the blindfolded "It" searches for a player to grab, the players are allowed to tease "It" by tickling, touching the arm, whispering, etc.)—all at the risk of being caught by "It."

Capture the Flag

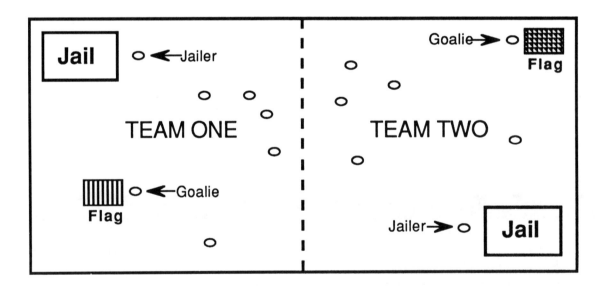

The playing area is set up as shown in the diagram on the next page.

Team One is on one side of the field, and Team Two is on the other side. A towel, bandanna, or rag is used for each team's flag. The idea of the game is to somehow capture the opposing team's flag, located in the other team's territory, without getting tagged. Once a player crosses over the line in the middle of the field, she can be tagged and sent to that team's "jail," which is set up anywhere within the team's boundaries. If a player lands in jail, one of his teammates can free him by getting to the jail without getting tagged. Any teammate who reaches the jail without being tagged can free all of the jailed players by tagging them. Both the tagger and the freed players get a free walk back to their side of the playing field.

Each team appoints one "goalie," who watches the flag from a distance of ten feet away, and one "jailer," who guards the jail. (You can also play a version that allows more than one player to guard the flag or jail.) A team may choose to leave the flag or the jail unguarded if they need more players to work out the team's strategy for capturing the opposing team's flag.

Cottontail Tag

Ask all the players to bring a can of shaving cream to the meeting. Give a Bull's-eye Belt" to each player. This consists of a square foot of cardboard with a circle drawn on it and a string strung through it long enough to go around a player's waist. Players tie their belts on with the cardboard in back where a tail would go. Split the players into two teams, and explain that the object of the game is to squirt a glob of shaving cream onto the bull's-eyes worn by members of the opposing team, while at the same time protecting their own targets. Players may not touch or sit down on their own bull's-eyes. To count as a "cotton tail," the shaving cream must stick to the cardboard and be inside the bull's-eye. The team that has successfully put the most cotton tails on the other team within the time limit is the winner.

Human Pac Man

Everybody is familiar with the popular video game Pac Man. Here's a way to convert it to active playing. On a large playing area like a gym floor, create a maze with chairs or masking tape (if outdoors, mark the field with chalk). At the four corners of the maze are "energizers" (one group used hymnbooks), and in the middle is an open space which is home base for the "ghosts." There is one Pac Man and up to four ghosts. (Use more ghosts if the maze is large.)

The rules for the game are as follows:

1. Stay in the maze.
2. Only one Pac Man. Rotate players into the game.
3. Pac Man moves by shuffling his feet along the floor. Feet should never leave the ground. (This is great fun to watch.)
4. Ghosts walk at a moderate pace. *No*

running. Safety guards can monitor this.

5. Ghosts move forward only and must follow the maze. No stopping.
6. Pac Man can go in any direction and may stop.
7. Pac Man's objective—to avoid being eaten by ghosts.
8. Ghost's objective—to eat the Pac Man.
9. Pac Man may tag ghosts only when energized (by picking up an energizer).
10. Pac Man is energized for only eight seconds (safety guard can keep time.)

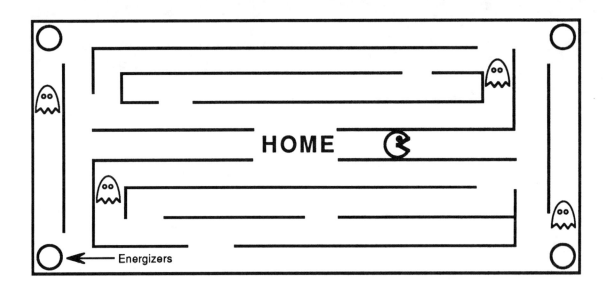

11. When eight seconds are up, Pac Man must put the energizer down wherever he is. He cannot carry it around longer than 8 seconds.
12. When the ghost is tagged, it must return to touch home base before returning to the game.
13. When Pac Man picks up an energizer, he must say, "Energize."
14. Ghosts must tag Pac Man with both hands.
15. Pac Man can tag ghosts with one hand while energized.
16 No reaching over the chairs or outside the maze passageway.
17. Pac Man starts each game by saying, "Pac Man, go."
18. Pac Man has three lives to a round.
19. Energizers are placed back in the corners at the end of each game.

Human Pac Man II

For this variation of "Human Pac Man," the players line up in rows as shown in the diagram. When one player (the caller) says, "Passageways," all players grab hands with the players standing next to them in one direction (e.g., horizontally). And when the caller says, "Corridors," the players turn ninety degrees the other way, grab hands, and form rows running the other direction (e.g., vertically). One person is Pac Man, and two people are ghosts. You will also need four tennis balls and someone to count (the counter).

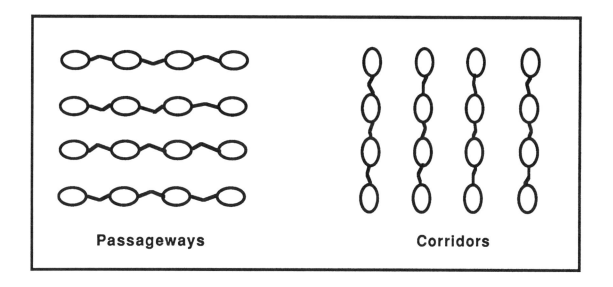

Passageways   **Corridors**

Place one tennis ball in each corner of the square (see diagram). Pac Man has three "lives" during which he tries to retrieve all four balls. He should start each turn from the center. Ghosts start each turn from any two diagonal corners; they should not be in the same corner.

The caller begins the game by calling passageways or corridors, and the people forming the square create the correct passage. Pac Man then walks towards any tennis ball, following the passageway or corridor. Pac Man may not reach over or under any arm to collect a ball. The ghosts, also following only the passageways or corridors, chase Pac Man. They may not hover around any ball, but must keep moving. They cannot stop. Ghosts can move only by hopping with both feet together (bunny hop).

Pac Man may also call passageways or corridors to create a route to the balls or to get out of a jam. But he may make a total of only ten calls throughout his three lives. The counter keeps track of

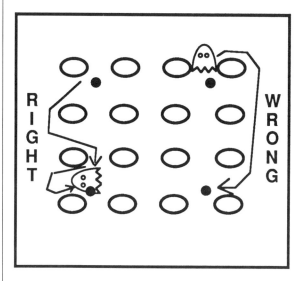

how many times Pac Man calls either passageways or corridors. If Pac Man uses ten calls on the first turn, for example, he can make no more calls for the rest of the game. A turn ends if Pac Man is tagged by one or both of the ghosts, or if he fails to follow the passageway or corridor, or if he collects all four balls. Should a ghost fail to follow a passageway or corridor, all players return to starting points to replay the turn. Pac Man gets to keep any balls he collected on that turn, however.

The caller calls, "Passageways," or "Corridors," every fifteen seconds or so, but waits two to three seconds after Pac Man uses one of his calls before changing again. The caller sets the pace by how often she makes a call. Pac Man and the ghosts may not run from corner to corner along the outside of the square, though they may go outside to get to another row. Allow all the players a chance to be Pac Man or a ghost. Feel free to change the rules or to adapt the game as you wish.

Human Pac Man III

Here's another relatively simple adaptation of the Pac Man video game. This one is best suited for more than fifty players. Divide your group into four teams and remove one player from each team. Form your maze with the remaining players, making the outside square as large as you desire the maze to be. On the inside form the maze by lining people up with arms outstretched to make walls and corners.

Now blindfold three of the four players you have selected. These are the "ghosts." The person without the blindfold is "Pac Man." Attach a balloon to the backs of all four. Pac Man is to chase after the three ghosts to try to burst their balloons. The ghosts are to try to burst the balloon of Pac Man. All four must move through the maze slowly, either by hopping or shuffling their feet. The players try to direct the ghosts by yelling directions to them. Give as many players as possible a chance to be inside the maze.

Hat and Go Seek

Here's a game that combines the best of tag and hide-and-go-seek. One person wears an old hat (she cannot merely carry it), hides her eyes, and gives the rest of the group a count of fifty to run and hide. Then the hat-wearer begins to search. When the hat-wearer finds and tags one of the players, that person must put on the hat, cover his eyes for twenty counts so the old "It" can hide, and then continue the search.

Kick the Cans

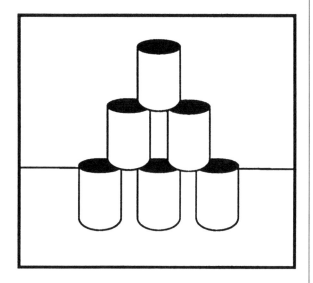

Six empty soft-drink cans, the dark cover of night, lots of places to hide, and a large area in which to play are the only requirements for this game that could last for hours. The hardest part is usually selecting the first person to be "It."

The six cans (bring extras in case these get bent) are stacked pyramid-style—three on the bottom, two on the next row, and one on top. Someone kicks the cans to start the game and while "It" is retrieving and restacking the cans, everyone hides.

The object of the game is simple: try to sneak up and kick the cans before "It" can call your name. "It" cannot just stand by the cans, however, but must look around for people hiding. "It" can go anywhere and can call people's names at any time she sees them as long as the cans are stacked. Any player whose name is called before kicking the cans goes to prison (create some sort of jailhouse near the cans). If someone kicks the cans, though, everybody previously caught is set free. Limit the number of kicks on any one person so no one is "It" all night. For example, if a person fails to catch everyone before ten kicks or fifteen minutes, someone else is chosen to be "It"—preferably someone who has not yet been "It." (Generally only large groups need the limits. "It" rotates more readily in groups of ten to twelve players.)

Laser Light Tag

The name alone will excite your young people. You will need one or more flashlights and a dark night for this one. Select one player (or more) to begin as "It." Players scatter around a defined play area that has many good hiding places. "It" counts to 100 while players hide.

"It" then searches for hidden players, attempting to tag them *above the shoulders* with a beam of light. Players can move from hiding place to hiding place. Players tagged with the light go directly to the "laser-light prison." Construct the prison by setting four flashlights so that they create a square prison of light. (Be sure to have extra flashlight batteries on hand.) Jailed players can escape only if they are tagged by a free player. Freed players get a thirty-second chance to hide before they can be tagged again. A safety guard needs to be available to make calls on disputed tags or escapes from prison. The last person tagged (or the last two or three) becomes the new "It."

In an indoor variation of this game, Duo Laser-Light Tag, two players are chosen to be "It." The other players hide in a darkened room that has been made safe, and the Laser-Light Duo attacks. The two players must simultaneously tag a player above the shoulders before that player must go to prison. There is no escape from prison. Players tagged by one beam of light can move out of the way before the other beam hits them. Alert safety guards to watch for the players' safety as well as to make calls on disputed tags.

Old-Sock Tag

This is an older child's version of the game A-Tisket, A-Tasket. The players form a circle with all players facing inward. One player is chosen to be "It" and given an old, clean sock to carry. "It" walks around the outside of the circle with the sock in hand. Suddenly and as shrewdly as possible, "It" drops the sock behind one of the players in the circle and begins to run. As soon as the player realizes the sock is behind him, that player must chase after "It" as fast as possible. The object of the game is for "It" to run completely around the circle back to the dropped sock and take the chasing player's place without getting tagged. If "It" is tagged, she remains "It." If "It" eludes being tagged, the chaser becomes the new "It."

Another version of this game is for the chaser to pick up the sock, begin chasing "It," and tag "It" by throwing the sock at her. If the chaser hits "It" with the sock, she remains "It." If the chaser fails to tag "It" with the sock, the chaser becomes the new "It." For added fun, use a white tube sock and fill it with a little cornstarch.

Prisoner-of-War Tag

For this game, you'll need a large playing field or area marked as shown in the diagram. At the front end of each section there needs to be a 4 x 4 area marked off as the prison.

Divide your group into two teams. Each team is allowed two minutes to huddle in their home turf and create a strategy of attack. A coin toss determines which team gets to send out the first player. The most important rule for players to remember is that a player can tag only opponents who left their home turf before that player did. And a player can only be tagged by opponents who left their home turf after that player did. Another important rule is that tagged players must go directly to prison, but can be released if touched by a player from their own team. After being freed a prisoner and the player freeing the prisoner get a free walk back to their home turf, and they must return to their home turf before they can begin tagging again. Only one prisoner can be freed at a time.

Play begins with the team who won the coin toss (Team One), sending out a player to challenge the other team. A player from the opposing team (Team

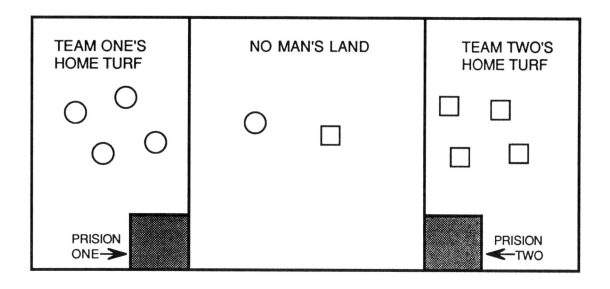

Two) then sends out a player to try to tag Team One's player. Team One can now send out another player to try to rescue their teammate, and so on. The tag bat-tle has begun. You'll need several safety guards to keep track of the mess. It is great fun.

Protection Tag

This is a great tag game that can be played indoors in a large, safe room free of obstacles. Divided the group into four teams that each huddle in one of the four corners of the playing room. Mark off the corners with masking tape as well as marking off a jail in the middle of the room. One player is chosen to be "It."

The object of this crazy tag game is for players to run from safety zone to safety zone (the four corners of the room) without getting tagged by "It." All tagged players must go to jail until everyone has been tagged. "It" must tag players with both hands.

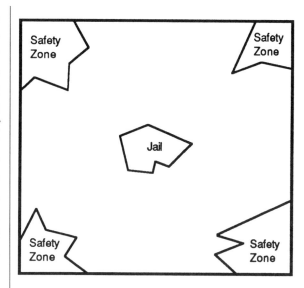

Radioactivity Tag

Decide upon the boundaries for this nuclear game of tag. Players hold hands in a circle with a radioactive particle (playground ball) placed in the middle. The group tries to pull one of the players towards the ball. The first player (or players; there can be more than one) to be forced to touch the ball becomes the "Radioactive It." "It" tries to tag as many players as possible. Any player tagged also becomes "Radioactive" and tries to tag other players. When everyone is tagged, another round can be played.

Shark in the Water

This tag game is similar to a favorite children's game, Pom, Pom, Pull Away. Two goal lines are marked about thirty to fifty feet apart on a safe, open playing surface. One player is chosen to be the "shark" and stands between the two goal lines. All the players then line up behind one of the goal lines. The shark calls out, "Shark in the water," and all the players must swim (run) to the opposite goal line. The shark tries to eat (tag) as many players as possible. Any player tagged also becomes a shark. When the untagged players reach the

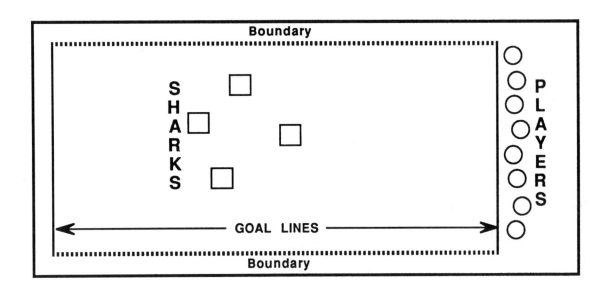

safety of the other goal line, the shark can again call out, "Shark in the water," and the players must again run to the other goal line, only this time they may have to avoid more than one shark. When all players have been tagged by the sharks, a new round can be played with the first or last person tagged becoming the new shark.

A variation of this game is to have tagged players become sharks, but remain standing in one place. They can tag players as they pass by, but they cannot move their feet.

Snatch the Bacon

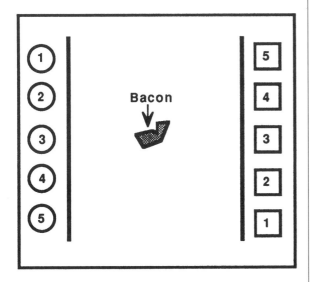

This is a great outdoor game. Divide the group into two teams, each lined up behind its goal line twenty to thirty feet apart. Place a handkerchief (or an old towel or sock) at a point half-way between goal lines. Each player is given a number with players on both teams having corresponding numbers. The two teams are numbered from opposite ends of the line so that the same numbered players face each other diago-

nally (except the two middle players, of course).

The leader calls out a number. The player on each team having that number runs to the center and tries to snatch the bacon (handkerchief) and return to her goal without being tagged by the other player. The more skilled players will run into the center and hover over the bacon until their opponent is off guard and they can snatch it and run. Each successful return gains two points for the returning team. If tagged, the tagging team gets one point. Obviously, it pays to successfully snatch the bacon. However, if a player can tag the snatcher, his team still gets a point.

After each return or tag, the bacon is placed back in the center, and another number is called. Play for a designated number of points. The leader should call numbers in a manner that creates suspense. Although all numbers should be included, repeat a number now and then to keep all players alert. Maintain interest by calling two or more numbers simultaneously, thereby involving four or more players at once.

Tape War

Set up a table at each end of the playing area, form a semicircular safety zone in front of each table with pylons or chairs (see diagram on the next page), and stick a bunch of two-inch-long pieces of masking tape to the front edge of each table (two pieces per team member). Have safety guards on each side to monitor activity in and out of the safety zones.

The game starts as both teams pile

into their own safety zones, grab one piece of tape each, and then enter the battle zone in order to stick the tape on their opponents' bodies below the shoulders. Players cannot remove the tape once they are stuck. After sticking someone players can return to their safety zone (for only ten seconds) for one more piece of tape.

After a specified period of time (keep it short), the game ends, teams count

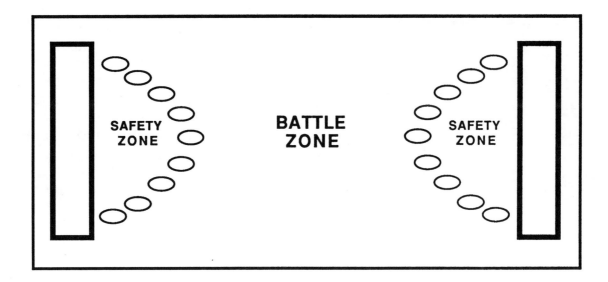

how many hits they have received, and the team with the least hits wins. Colored tape gives the game a brighter aspect. Use it to designate teams.

Time-Warp Tag

Here's another crazy version of the most famous of all games. You simply play a regular game of tag, but at the blow of a whistle, each player (including "It") must slow down to a speed equal to a sports replay "slo-mo." In other words, they must do everything in slow motion. Players will soon get the hang of it and become very exaggerated in their motions.

Make sure the players do everything in "time warp" state, even talking and shouting. The game can be played in total time warp, or you can blow the whistle for start/stop intervals. Limit the size of the play area so that several players have a chance to become "It."

Trio Tag

The group needs to be divided into threesomes. One of the three is chosen to be "It" (draw straws). A simple game of tag is now played between, and only between, the trio. When "It" tags one of the two players on that team, there is a five-second "no touch backs" period.

Players need to be confined to a specified playing area. The fun of this simple tag game is to dodge and hide behind players from other teams. The game ends when everyone drops from exhaustion or is ready to move to another game or activity.

Ultimate Elimination

If you have thirty or more kids and a big playing field, this tag-ball game can continue for a long, exciting time. Players should pair off and tie themselves together at the arm. Throw into the fray several Frisbees (foam version) or Nerf balls—or a combination of them—and it's every pair for itself. When one person of a pair is hit, he can no longer throw, but can only defend his partner. When his partner is hit as well, that pair is out of the game altogether—that is, until the pair that finally eliminated them is itself eliminated. Then the first pair can join the game again.

Just when you think the game is winding down, a lethal pair that eliminated several other pairs is itself eliminated—and competition picks up quickly as those renewed pairs can play again.

Water-Balloon Boppers

Here's a new way to have a water balloon war. Have everyone bring a regular sock to use—long tube socks work the best. Then give each person a water balloon to put inside the sock.

Now have a water balloon fight in which players try to "tag" each other with their water-balloon boppers. If a player's water balloon breaks, she is out of the game, but if players can hit someone without breaking their water balloons, then they can remain in the game to hit someone else. Allow tagging only from the shoulders down.

A variation of this game is to eliminate anyone who gets tagged as well as anyone whose water balloon breaks. Either way it's lots of fun.

Zimbat

This game is very similar to the old game Capture the Flag (page 32). Two teams are situated on a large playing field with a boundary dividing the field in half. Each team is given a flag, which they must place in a conspicuous position and protect. When a team captures the flag of the opposing team by taking it over to their side of the field, they win. Players tagged while in the enemy's territory are captured and sent to jail. The jail is a designated area deep in a team's territory.

So far, it's just like regular Capture the Flag. But this game differs through the addition of Frisbees (use the foam disk variety). About a fourth of the players are issued Frisbees. Any player tagged by a Frisbee, whether it is thrown or held, is sent to prison, regardless of which side of the field they are on.

Additional rules include:
- Jailed players stay in jail two minutes, and then they are automatically free. There is no freeing prisoners as in regular Capture the Flag.
- A Frisbee must be "dead" in order for someone to pick it up. Anyone still in the game may pick up a dead frisbee regardless of who threw it.
- Jailed players must surrender their Frisbees to the nearest person.

Outrageous Circle Games

Check out these outrageous circle games for a roundabout way to play.

Anatomy Shuffle

The group pairs off and forms two concentric circles—one member of each couple in the inner circle, the other in the outer circle.

The outer circle begins traveling clockwise, while the inner circle goes counter-clockwise. When the leader blows a whistle (or yells, "Anatomy shuffle") and calls out, "Hand-ear," the outer circle stops, and the kids in the inner circle must find their partners and place their hands on their partner's ears. The last pair to do so is out. The first body part called is what the inner-circle kids must touch to the proper

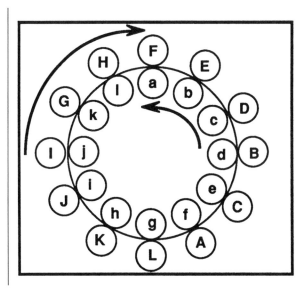

body part of their partners. The second body part called is what the kids in the outer circle touch with their partners from the inner circle. The leader calls out all sorts of combinations such as:

Finger-foot
Nose-shoulder
Wrist-knee
Thigh-thigh
Head-stomach
Foot-head
Elbow-nose
Nose-armpit
Back-back

If you want an even wilder game, allow both members of each pair to scramble for each other when the whistle blows and the match is announced. The last pair to remain in the game wins.

Blackout

Here's a new twist to musical chairs that is a real riot. First, in a play area free of obstacles, arrange the chairs in a circle facing outward. Players form a circle around the outside of the chairs, keeping their hands behind their backs. Have half the group walk around the chairs clockwise and the other half move counter-clockwise when the music starts or when the whistle blows. When the music stops, participants must sit down on the closest empty chair available. There is one catch: the game is played in the dark. When the music starts, have someone turn the lights out. When the music stops, the lights go back on. Be prepared for a lot of scrambling, screaming, and running for chairs. The person left standing is out. Be sure to take one chair out after each round, and move the remaining chairs closer together as the group gets smaller. And make sure the lights go on when the music stops for obvious safety reasons.

Chair-Ball Confusion

Have the group sit in a circle, either in chairs or on the floor. "It" sits in the middle of the circle on a sturdy chair or stool. Members sitting in the outer circle

pass a foam ball, sponge, or other safe ball (a soft or partially deflated volleyball works) around the circle. The ball or other soft object should be thrown around the circle until "It" is confused.

Suddenly, any player in the circle throws the ball at the chair or stool occupied by "It." The job of "It" is to defend the chair or stool, not allowing the ball to hit any part of the chair or stool. If "It" succeeds in the defense, she remains "It" for another round. If the shot hits the chair or stool, the player who scored the successful shot switches places with "It," and the game continues for another round. It's more fun not to keep score.

If the group is large, break into two or three smaller teams and rotate into the middle as "It" players from each of the competing teams. Three outs for a team's "It," and another team gets to rotate their chosen "It" into the circle.

Dice Dive

Here's a wild living-room game for small groups. For larger groups, divide into smaller groups and get several games going at once. Ask players to sit in a circle and number off (one, two, one, two) so that every other player is on the opposite team. Place a pile of marbles on the floor in one big mass in the center of the circle of kids. There should be about six to ten marbles per player. (Pennies can also be used.)

Any player begins by throwing a pair of dice onto the floor. If the total is *even*, nothing happens. But if the total is *odd*, everyone must dive to the marbles and grab as many as possible until all of them are gone. Points are totaled (one point for each marble grabbed by a team), and the marbles are returned to the pile. Now a player on the opposing team throws the dice. Turns alternate between team members this way until everyone has had a chance to throw. Then the game is over, and the team with the biggest total wins.

If anyone grabs the marbles when the dice throw is *even* (it will happen frequently), all marbles grabbed must be deducted from the offending team's total at that point. The game gets rather frantic as players try to anticipate the roll of the dice, so it's a good idea to have players clip their fingernails before the game to avoid scratches. It's a good idea to make a circle around the marbles with chalk, masking tape, or string, and tell everyone stay behind that line until the dice hit the floor.

Earth, Air, Fire, Water

Players form a circle with "It" in the center. "It" throws a ball (or any soft, safe object) to a person in the circle, quickly says either earth, air, fire, or water, and then counts to ten rapidly (the element of surprise is important here). The person who receives the ball must respond by naming an animal according to the category chosen before "It" finishes her count. If "It" chooses earth, the player must name an animal that lives on dry land; if air, an animal that flies; if water, an animal that lives in the water; and if fire, the player says nothing. If a person responds incorrectly, he takes "It's" place. Players cannot duplicate an answer already given—each answer must be an original.

Flat Tire

This great outdoor game can be played with small or large groups. Scatter old tires around the playing field, one tire for every two people. (Many tire centers will give you their old tires, especially if they know they will be put to good use with young people.) It's more fun if you can get an assortment of tire sizes.

Two people stand in each tire. "It" stands in the middle of all the scattered tires. When "It" yells out, "Flat tire," everyone in the tires must exchange places. During the switch, "It" attempts to jump into a tire. Whoever is left without a tire is the new "It."

To vary the game, name groups of kids White Walls, Snow Tires, Radials, Steel-belts, etc. Remember to give "It" a name, too. "It" then has the option of calling out one or more names. Those people then must exchange tires. "It" again attempts to get her own tire. In this version, as in the last, "Flat Tire" means everyone must run for a new tire.

Garbage-Bag Ball

For this game fill a large plastic garbage bag with blown-up balloons, and tie it with a twist-tie. You now have a "garbage-bag ball." All but ten of the kids form a large circle on their knees. The ten kids then form a pinwheel in the center of the circle, lying on their backs, heads toward the center. Everyone should have their shoes off for best results. The garbage-bag ball is then tossed into the circle. The object is for the kids on their backs to kick or hit the ball out of the circle, over the heads of the kids in the outer circle. The outer circle tries to keep it in play. Play for as long as you wish, or try this variation: if the ball is kicked over a player's head in the outer circle, then he must take the place of the person in the inner circle who kicked it.

Group Juggle

This circle game is something like Hot Potato with a dash of Concentration. Throw a ball to one person in a standing circle of young people. The person catching it throws it to another, and so on until everyone has received and thrown the ball once—but exactly once. No one should get the ball a second time, which means each player needs to remember where the ball's been. If your group's frustration threshold and skill-level are high, increase the speed of the game and add more balls. If your group is having difficulty with this game, break into smaller circles with fewer people.

Hot Towel

Here's a good, active indoor circle game. Everyone sits in a circle with one person in the center of the circle as "It."

"It" tosses a knotted towel to someone sitting in the circle, and then the towel is passed around the circle in any direction. The object of the game is for "It" to tag the player who is holding the towel *while it is in the towel holder's possession*. When "It" tags someone with the towel, they exchange places. If "It" catches the towel, the thrower becomes "It." If a bad throw is made and "It" grabs the towel, whoever made the bad throw becomes the new "It."

Murder

To start this great indoor game, place one slip of paper for each player in a hat. On one of these slips of paper write "detective," and on another "murderer." The rest of them are blank. Everyone draws a slip from the hat. Whoever drew the word "detective" announces himself, and it is his job to locate the murderer, who tries not to give herself away. From this point there are two ways the game can be played.

1. The detective leaves the room, and the room is darkened. While all the players mill about the room, the murderer silently slips up behind someone and very quietly whispers in his ear, "You're dead." The victim counts to three, screams, and falls to the floor. The lights are turned on and the detective re-enters the room. He questions the players for one minute (or so) and tries to guess the identity of the murderer. If the detective is correct, the murderer becomes the detective, and a new murderer is selected. During the questioning, only the murderer may lie. All others must tell the truth about what, if anything, they saw.

2. The detective remains in the room, and the murderer attempts to "murder" as many victims as possible (in the manner described above) before getting caught by the detective.

Everyone should get a chance to play both roles if time permits. Murder is best played with at least fifteen people.

Musical Hats

This game gives Musical Chairs a new twist. The group stands in a circle, each facing the back of the person in front. All but one person put on hats (they can be paper-bag hats), and on a signal or when the music starts, all players grab the hats on the heads of the people in front of them and put them on. Players continue moving hats from head to head around the circle until the music stops. Whoever is left without a hat when the music stops is out of the game. Remove one hat, and repeat the hat exchange until only two people are left. The last two players stand back to back, grabbing the hat off of each other's heads until the music stops. The one with the hat on is the winner.

Newspaper Puzzle

Give a group of players seated in a tight circle a complete daily newspaper that you have thoroughly-but-neatly mixed up ahead of time. At the whistle give the kids the newspaper to reassemble in order as fast as they can. Keep the group as close together as possible since this makes it more difficult to reassemble properly.

Ojii-San to Obaa-San

In this Japanese game players sit in a circle. Two rolled-up kerchiefs are given to any two players in the circle who are seated some distance apart. These players loosely tie the kerchiefs around their necks. One kerchief represents the grandmother (Ojii-san), and the other kerchief represents the grandfather (Obaa-san). The object of the game is for the grandmother to chase and catch the grandfather. Here's how it works. When the leader says, "Go!" the two players with the kerchiefs around their necks clap their hands once, pull the kerchiefs off, and pass them to the players on their right who tie the kerchief on their necks, clap their hands once, and pass the kerchief to the right. This process continues until someone gets caught with the grandmother kerchief before they succeed in passing the grandfather kerchief on to the next player. Then play begins again.

Paddle Surprise

Players form a standing circle, straddling their legs so that their feet touch the feet of both players on either side. They may not move their feet during the game. "It" stands in the middle of the circle with a playground ball and tries to

roll the ball through the legs of the players standing around the circle. "It" can only use her hands to paddle or roll the ball through the legs of the other players. Neither "It" nor any other player can kick the ball. The ball must leave the circle in between the legs of one of the players standing in the circle in order for it to count. Players can stop the ball by paddling the ball with their hands. They can not move their feet to stop the ball. When the ball does roll through the straddled legs of a player, that player becomes the new "It" and play resumes.

Rattlesnake

For this game of stealth and skill, you will need two blindfolds, a small plastic bottle with a rock in it as a rattler (a prescription bottle works fine), a circle of players, and a referee. The referee blindfolds two players and places them inside the circle. One is designated the rattlesnake, and the other is the hunter. The referee spins the hunter several times so he loses his sense of direction (but not so much that he becomes sick). The group is now ready to begin play. It is essential that everyone remains absolutely quiet, either seated in a circle surrounding the two players or sitting around the edges of the defined playing area. When the referee says, "Rattlesnake," the blindfolded rattlesnake must shake her "rattler," and then try to escape capture by the hunter. The game continues with the referee periodically saying, "Rattlesnake!" until the hunter captures the rattlesnake. Pick two new people to blindfold and begin again.

Run 'n' Wet

To play this game your kids need to dress in swim suits and sit in a circle around a plump water balloon. Ask them to number themselves off. When you call out two numbers, those two kids must jump up, run around the circle back to their own place, and without stopping race through the empty spot they left to the water balloon in the middle. Can you guess the rest? Yup. The first one there gets to throw the balloon at the loser, who must stand still and not dodge it.

Sesame-Street Pong

For this game the players all hold a book with both hands and stand in a circle. One player uses her book to hit a ping-pong ball across the circle while calling out the letter A. The person on the other side hits it to someone while calling out the letter B, and so forth. The whole circle works together to see how far down the alphabet they can get before they blow it. There is no particular order for hitting the ball. Anyone can hit it when it comes to them, but no one may hit the ball twice in a row. (You can also break the circle into teams with every other person being on the same team. Players can only hit the ball to another team member. It's a real challenge!)

Shuffle Your Buns

Arrange chairs in a circle so that everyone has a chair. Choose one person to remove his chair and stand in the middle of the circle as "It." "It" calls out, "Shuffle your buns to the right," and everyone who is seated must move to the right from chair to chair, all the while trying to keep "It" from sitting down. "It" can also call out, "Shuffle your buns to the left," and the group must switch directions. When "It" does manage to get a seat, the person to his right becomes the new "It."

For a new twist to the game have two people become "It" at the same time with two empty chairs in the circle. This works well, especially for larger groups.

Squeak, Bunny, Squeak

Here's a fun game for smaller groups. Seat everyone in a circle of chairs. One person is chosen to be "It," and must stand in the middle of the circle. She is blindfolded and given a pillow. While the leader spins "It" around twice, the players seated in the circle change chairs. "It" must now locate a person, place the pillow on that person's lap and sit on it and say, "Squeak, Bunny, Squeak." The person who is being sat on disguises his voice and squeaks while "It" tries to guess whose lap she is sitting on. If the guess is correct, the person who is identified becomes the new "It." Some possible variations include:

• Instead of saying, "Squeak, Bunny, Squeak," you can substitute sayings like "Gobble, Turkey, Gobble," "Growl, Tiger, Growl," or "Cluck, Chicken, Cluck."

- Instead of using a pillow, "It" stays in the center of the circle and points to someone. That someone must leave the circle and stand in front of "It" who then says, "Squeak, Bunny, Squeak."

- "It" walks around the circle after being spun, touches someone on the head and says, "Squeak, Bunny, Squeak."

Swat

The group sits or stands in a circle, facing inward, with a wastebasket turned bottom-up in the center of the circle. One person is chosen to be "It" and stands inside the circle with a rolled-up newspaper (keep the roll soft enough so that it remains safe). "It" walks around the inside of the circle and swats one person on or below the knee. "It" must then race back to the wastebasket, place the newspaper on it, and return to the swatted person's place in the circle. This must be done before the swatted person is able to grab the newspaper from the wastebasket and hit "It" back. If the newspaper falls off the wastebasket, "It" must put the paper back on the wastebasket before running to the circle. If the swatted person is able to swat "It" before "It" reaches the empty place in the circle, "It" must return to the middle for another round. If the swatted person is unable to swat "It" back, the swatted person becomes the new "It" and play continues.

Tetherball Jump

Here's a classic game that kids really go for. Have ten to twenty kids form a circle. The leader gets in the center of the circle with a tether ball (a ball attached to a rope about eight feet long). The leader takes the rope in hand and spins, making a circle with the ball about six inches off the ground. The circle of kids moves in closer, and each person must jump over the ball as it passes by. The leader keeps going around and around with the ball, getting faster and faster until one of the players goofs. That person is then out (for thirty seconds or for the remainder of the round, depending upon how competitive you wish the game to be), and the game continues. As the game progresses you can make the ball go faster and/or higher off the ground. Alternate leaders when one gets too dizzy. Changing the spinning direction also helps.

Toss the Rag

Tie a rag or sock into a tight knot. Seat everyone in a circle with "It" in the middle. "It" tosses the rag to someone and shouts some category (soft drinks, washing machines, presidents, birds, books of the Bible, etc.). "It" counts to ten rapidly (or whatever number works for your group). If "It" reaches ten before the other person names an example of that category (Coke, Kenmore, Lincoln, Sapsucker, Ezekiel, etc.), then that person becomes the new "It" and switches places with the old "It." The category named should be a common noun, while the examples given should be proper nouns. If the person with the rag names a category before "It" gets to ten, then "It" tosses the rag to someone else, shouting out another category, and counting to ten.

Wet Sponge

This outdoor get-acquainted game works best with a group of at least thirty, but can be played with smaller groups. Have the group make a fairly large circle (about an arm's length from each other). In the center place a large bucket of water. Either four players or four adult leaders start out as "It." Each person who is "It" gets a sponge soaked with water and runs up to a different person in the circle and says, "Wet Sponge." That person answers, "Take a Plunge," to which "It" responds, "Who's a Grunge?" The person in the circle then names another person in the circle. The person with the sponge then runs up to that person and hits them with the soaked sponge. The person that was hit is now "It." The game goes very rapidly and ends when everyone is soaked or water is gone.

Sure-To-Please
Action Games

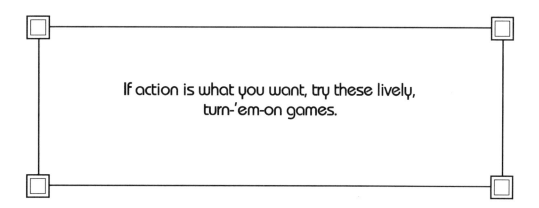

If action is what you want, try these lively,
turn-'em-on games.

Balloon Smash

All players tie a blown-up balloon around their waists so that the balloon hangs behind their back ends at least a foot. Each player also receives a soft, rolled-up newspaper. The object of the game is to break everyone else's balloon while keeping your own from being popped. Newspapers are the only weapon allowed. Safety guards should be scattered throughout the playing area. Emphasize that players must aim their newspapers at the balloons. No intentional striking of other players is allowed.

Big, Bad Wolf

Give three-player teams enough newspaper and tape to build a newspaper shelter of some kind. It must be big enough to get all three team members inside. The wolf or wolves (adult leaders) then attempt to blow the shelter down. Afterwards, have a giant paper fight.

Biggest Frog in the Pond

Place a large piece of newsprint in the center of a playing area free of any potentially hazardous obstacles. Divide your group in two—one group on the newsprint (the pond), the other surrounding it. Players squat on their feet

pretending they are frogs. The object of the game is to get into the pond. Players must remain in a squat position at all times. For a player to get on the newsprint, he must first remove a player from the newsprint.

Bubble Head

For this simple game, two players stand facing each other about four feet apart. Blow up a round balloon and have one player bump the balloon off his head to the other player. The second player bounces the balloon off her head back to the first player, and so on back and forth. See how many times they can bounce it without dropping it, using only their heads. Vary the distance to change the level of difficulty. Each player can move only the left foot while attempting to hit the balloon. The right foot must remain planted. Each player may pivot on the ball of the right foot, but no jumping is allowed.

A challenging variation of this game is for the two players to take a half a step back after each successful hit. Both players continue moving back, which increases the difficulty of the game.

Another variation is line teams up, spacing players about four feet apart. Each team must bounce a balloon all the way down the team line, from one head to the other. Again, right feet must remain planted. If a balloon is dropped the team must start over again.

Dice Grab

To play this game buy some oversized dice at a game or stationary store. If you want to make your own, cut two small blocks of wood into 1¼ inch cubes. Sand and paint them, and mark them with dots similar to a pair of dice.

Mark a circle two feet in diameter with chalk on the floor or a rug. Have the players sit around the circle. Break the group into two teams by counting one, two, one, two, one, two around the circle of players. One person from a team starts the game by rolling the dice toward the center and simultaneously calling out any single number between two and twelve. If the dots total the number called, all may grab for the dice. Each die is worth one point on the grab, and the scramble may continue out of the circle as long as the play area is safe. The game becomes more exciting as the time between throws is cut down. The roller continues until the number she calls is thrown, then she passes the dice to an adjacent player from the other team. Players should not be allowed a second turn as roller until all players on a team have had a chance to roll. A game is usually won when a team accumulates eleven points.

Electric Fence

For this game you need two poles and a piece of string. The string is tied between the two poles, about two feet off the floor at first. Play this game on a soft, safe carpet.

Divide into teams. The object of the game is for the entire team to get over the "electric fence" (the string) without getting "electrocuted" (touching the string). Each team takes a turn with team members going over one at a time. Even though one player goes over the rope at a time, that player's team members can help any way they want. Once a person is over the fence, however, she cannot come back around to help anyone. That means the last person from the team to cross the string must somehow get over without help on one side. This game requires lots of teamwork and cooperation.

After each team has successfully gotten over the string, that round is complete, and the string is raised a little

higher, as in regular high jump competition. Eventually whole teams are eliminated, because if one member of the team touches the fence, the entire team is eliminated. Or you can allow players to get three touches before their team is eliminated. As much as possible, evenly divide the teams according to height, age, and sex.

Geometry

This game requires some advance preparation. Cut out an equal number of circles, squares, and triangles (nine inches by nine inches is sufficient, but you can make them bigger). You will need as many shapes as you have players, minus one.

Scatter equal numbers of circles, squares, and triangles around a defined playing area. Each player chooses a shape and stands on it. Choose one player to begin the game as "It," or begin the game yourself. "It" should not have a shape. "It" calls out the name of one, two, or three shapes. Players standing on the shape or shapes called must run to stand on another shape. If "It" calls out, "Geometry," all players must relocate. The player first touching a shape is the one allowed to occupy that shape. Safety guards can act as referees in disputes over which player reached a shape first. While the players are scrambling to a new shape, "It" also runs and stands on an unoccupied shape. Whoever is left without a shape to stand on becomes "It."

Play goes something like this: "It" calls out, "Circles," and all players standing on circles must run and stand on other circles. "It" stands on the closest unoccupied circle she sees. The player left without a circle to stand on is now the new "It." The new "It" calls out "Geometry," and all the players rush to find any new shape. In the scramble if "It" is unable to get to a shape before another player, "It" then remains "It" for the next round.

Indoor Treasure Hunt

Twenty-five objects are placed in plain sight in various places around the room or rooms available. (If in a home, use several rooms.) Attached to each object is a number. Each person is given a list (like the one below); the idea is to be the first to find the objects on the list and write in the numbers attached. No one can move or touch an object when it is found, but must simply record the number attached to it. A sample list:

1. Skateboard _____
2. Earring _____
3. Stick of gum _____
4. Sock _____
5. Button _____
6. Spoon _____
7. Paper clip _____
8. Baseball _____
9. White string _____
10. Frisbee _____
11. Bible _____
12. A plant _____
13. Fly swatter _____
14. Penny _____
15. Dime _____
16. Candy _____
17. Bracelet _____
18. Comb _____
19. School book _____
20. Bat _____
21. Ring _____
22. Poster _____
23. Child's toy _____
24. Video _____
25. Door key _____

Inversion

This game requires a great deal of teamwork. It can be played as a competitive game (teams competing against each other) or as a cooperative game (everyone is on the same team).

Draw two parallel lines on the floor

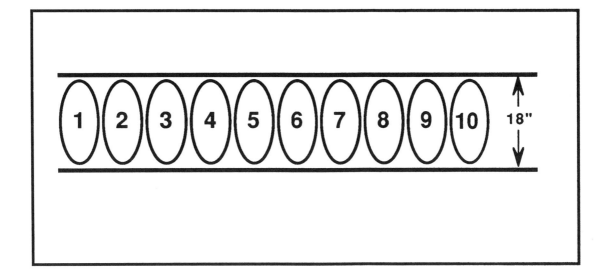

about eighteen inches apart. The team lines up inside those two lines. They number off consecutively from one end of the line to the other. On a signal they must reverse their order without stepping outside those two parallel lines. If there are ten people on the team, then player number one must change places with player number ten, and so on. Only the person in the middle stays in the same place.

Let the teams practice this once and come up with a strategy for doing it quickly and accurately. Then compete against the clock (try to set a "world record"), or see which team can do it in the quickest time. It's a lot of fun to watch. Safety guards can referee, adding a second to the team's time for every person on the team who steps outside one of the two lines. For a more challenging version bring the lines closer together.

Kleenex Blow

Have the players get into groups of between two and four. Each group receives a Kleenex (or any other brand) tissue, and they must keep the tissue in the air by blowing it. Players are not allowed to touch it. If a player touches the tissue, he must get it back into play by throwing it into the air. Time each group to see how long they are able to keep a tissue flying without touching.

Mad Hatter

Here's a free-for-all game that is really wild. Remember to have several safety guards on patrol for this one. Give players a paper bag "hat" to wear over their heads down to their ears and a "club" (a sock stuffed full of cloth or something soft). When the signal is given, everybody tries to knock off everybody else's hat while keeping their own on. No hands may be used. Players may not knock off the hat with anything but the cloth club. When a player's hat falls off, she must remain in the "Mad Hatter's Jail" (any sort of boundaried area away from play) for one minute. Have one of your safety guards watch the jail. Set a time limit for play and have fun.

Monster Bubbles

Kids have always loved bubbles. Here's a great recipe for giant bubbles that can be used for any number of games and activities. Mix in a bucket or tub one part liquid dish soap to three parts water. Add more water or liquid detergent depending on how large you want the bubbles and how soon you want them to pop. For additional staying power, add some glycerine, which can be purchased at many grocery or craft-supply stores.

You can make your own personalized bubble hoop by running a string through two plastic drinking straws. Make the hoop as large as you like, and then dunk it into the bucket or tub of solution. Before you lift the hoop out, put the straws right next to each other. As you lift the hoop out, slowly draw the straws apart. You may have to walk backwards slowly, swinging the hoop with your arms to have a bubble form. Practice at home before you do it with your group of kids. It takes some practice before you are able to get the real big bubbles going. Have enough supplies so that each of your kids can make their own personalized bubble hoop. Remember, however, that "a windy day doth not a bubble make."

Paper-Airplane Derby

Create several work stations around with room with different kinds and colors of paper, paints, and glue. Randomly place the kids and your adult workers into groups of threes. Let every group come up with their own paper airplane made out of paper, paint, and glue only (no wire, paper clips, wood, etc.). Give awards to every group for things like farthest flight, plane that stayed in the air the longest, most creative-looking plane, craziest plane, etc.

Scat

Here's an old game that children have been playing for a long time, but may be new to some of your kids. Assign everyone a number, leaving two mystery numbers not assigned to anyone. The player beginning as "It" is given a playground ball or other large, safe ball to throw at the other players.

"It" throws the ball in the air and calls a number. Everyone scatters except the person whose number was called. The player whose number was called is now "It" and must immediately retrieve the ball and yell, "Scat!" All players must stop scattering and freeze in their tracks. The new "It" then takes four giant steps toward another player while shouting out the four letters "S-C-A-T." "It" tries to hit that player below the waist with the ball. If that player is hit, he receives a letter (S, C, A, or T), and becomes the new "It." If the thrower misses, then the thrower gets a letter.

If one of the mystery numbers is called, then all players get a letter. Peo-ple who get all four letters, S-C-A-T, are eliminated from either the rest of the game or from one minute of play, after which they return to play with no let-ters.) After each round of play, players gather around "It," who has the ball, and play resumes.

If you wish to add a little more diffi-culty to the game, require that players who are "It" bounce the ball as hard as they can on the ground while calling out a number. Bouncing the ball makes it more difficult to retrieve. The game is best played in an outdoor playground area. If you wish to play indoors, use a foam ball, do not allow "It" to take any steps toward a player, and remove all potentially hazardous objects from the area of play.

Tail Grab

Divide the group into any number of equal "chains" (a line of people in which each person grips the wrist of the one in front of her). The last person in the chain has a handkerchief or scarf "tail" dan-gling behind him. The object is for each front person to snatch the tail from another line. The tail cannot be tied to a player's clothing. The fun is trying to maneuver to get someone else's tail while trying to protect your own. The safety guards should watch for chains trying to play "crack the whip" or mov-ing their chain so fast that someone could get hurt.

A variation of this game is to have the players grab the waist rather than the wrist of the person in front of them. This helps to slow the game down a bit.

Train Wreck

Arrange chairs in two straight lines with an aisle down the middle. The chairs should all be facing forward in the same direction. Number each chair in order by placing a piece of masking tape with a number printed on it on the seats of all the chairs.

Have all players except a "conductor" seated. There should be no extra chairs. The conductor stands in front and calls out seven numbers before yelling, "Train wreck!" The people seated in chairs with the numbers called must exchange seats with each other. The conductor also must scramble to find an empty seat. The person left without a chair is the new conductor. A conductor can yell, "Train wreck," without calling any numbers, which means everyone seated must exchange chairs.

Water Baggees

Water balloon fights have always been associated with childhood fun. But it takes time to fill up the balloons. One alternative is to have buckets of water ready and a supply of Zip-loc plastic sandwich bags. As the throwing gets underway, the participants fill the bags by hiding them under water and closing the top. The result is an instant, very temporary, water balloon substitute. Another advantage is that cleanup is easier than with regular water balloons.

CHAPTER

The Best Races and Relays

Looking for a game to get your group on the move?
These may be just the games you need. There is nothing
like a great relay or race to get kids excited!

Back-To-Back Relay

This is a variation of the old "three-legged race." Rather than trying two people side by side, you instead tie two people together back to back. One of them runs forward, and the other runs backward. When the two players reach the finish line, instead of turning around to run back, the one who ran forward now runs backward. Players should be tied loosely together at the waist with a rope or belt, or players can connect by interlocking their arms while back to back. When one pair finishes, the next pair goes. The first team to finish is the winner.

Balloon-Pop Relay

Divide the group into teams. The teams line up single file at a starting line. A chair is placed about thirty feet in front of the lines. Each team member has a deflated balloon. One at a time players run to the chair, blow up a balloon, tie it, pop it by sitting on it, and go to the end of the team line. The first team to pop all of its balloons wins. (If your kids are a little young for tying balloons, station an adult leader by each chair to tie for that team.)

Basketball Pass

In this simple relay two teams with an equal number of players line up single file in two lines. The player at the front of each line has a basketball (or several basketballs). The front player passes the ball over her head to the player behind her. The next player passes it between his legs to the player behind him, and so on. The ball(s) continues to the end of the line going over and under. After a player passes the ball, he sits down. Time the teams to see who can move the ball the fastest.

Blind Relay

Teams form two parallel lines for this relay. The players at the front of each team's line are blindfolded. About ten to fifteen feet away from the lines, widely scatter as many objects as there are players—objects must be things that can be safely carried by blind-folded players. To start the game call out the name of one of the objects scattered around the play area. The two blind-folded players, carrying a bag in their hands, crawl on their knees to the objects. The blind-folded players are to locate an object, place it in their bags, and return to their team lines. A team can help their player locate an object by verbally directing her. The team can also try to confuse their opponents through verbal misdirections.

Blind Wheelbarrow Race

This game is as much fun to watch as it is to play. You need two large wheelbarrows, two identical obstacle courses, and three people on each team. One person rides inside the wheelbarrow and is the navigator. The other two are the motors and are blindfolded. Each of the blindfolded motors takes one handle of the wheelbarrow and pushes the wheelbarrow through the obstacle

course, following the directions of the navigator. Be ready for some crashes and spills! You can run heats to determine the winner, or you can use a stopwatch to determine the best time. Be sure to play this game on a soft grass field.

Blow-Cup Relay

Put a hole in the bottom of a paper cup and thread it on a piece of string fifteen feet long (see illustration). Give one prepared string to each team. The string is held taut so the cup can slide, and the paper cup is placed at one end of the string. The teams line up single file at the end where the paper cup is. At the signal each player must blow the cup to the other end of the string (with hands behind back), and then push it back to the start for the next player on his team. The first team whose members all finish wins.

Blow-Cup Relay II

Here's a variation of the Blow-Cup Relay. Wrap two Styrofoam cups together, bottom to bottom, punch a hole in the center of the two connected bottoms, and thread them onto a piece of string. Connect the string to two stationary objects and pull it taut. Each team lines up, half on one end of the string and half on the other end.

The first person blows the cup along

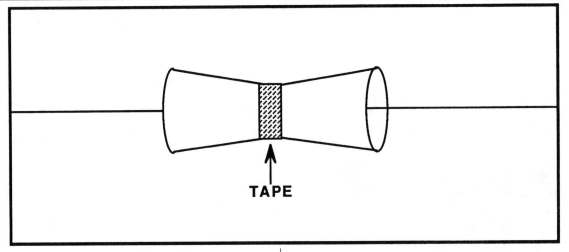

TAPE

the string to the other end, and the first person on that end blows it back to the other end, and so on until everyone has gone. The first team to finish is the winner. You will need a string and cup for each team if they compete all at once. Or you can have the teams go one at a time and simply time them with a stopwatch.

Another way to do this is to have two teams line up on each end of the string. The cup is positioned in the middle. On "Go!" the first two players run out to the center and start blowing, trying to out-blow their opponent. When the whistle is blown, they stop, run back to their teams, and two new players take over wherever the other two leave the cup. The object is to blow the cup as far as possible into the other team's "territory." The game ends when the cup reaches one end of the string or after all the players have had their turn. The team that blows the cup into their opponent's territory wins the game.

Bumper-Box Relay

For this relay obtain a large refrigerator box for each team. The first player for each team then gets inside the box, standing up with the box over his head and the open end of the box down to the floor. On a signal the players inside the boxes race to the opposite goal and back guided by their teammates, who must yell directions from behind the starting line. Since the players cannot see, they will bump into each other, go the wrong way, and the results are really funny. For an added dimension decorate the boxes with wild colors, team names, or whatever. This game should be played outside in a safe area free of obstacles. Assign a safety guard to each of the boxes, and have the guard walk with the player during the relay race.

Chewing-Gum Relay

This relay race for two or more teams uses sticks of chewing gum, work gloves, and shopping bags. Individually wrapped sticks of gum are placed inside the shopping bags (at least one stick per player). One shopping bag per team is placed at a goal line twenty feet away from the teams' starting line. Each team is given a pair of work gloves. The idea is for one player to put on the gloves, run down to the bag, pull out a piece of gum, unwrap it with the gloves on, and chew it while running back and passing the gloves to the next person. This is a fun relay to watch as well as to play.

Cotton-Ball Race

For this indoor relay game divide into teams of four, six, or twelve, and provide each team with a number of cotton balls in a container (such as a dish or pan). Each team also gets a spatula and an egg carton.

On a signal the first person on each team picks up a cotton ball with a spat-ula and tries to balance it on the spatula while running to a goal and back. If they go too fast, they will lose the cotton ball and must start over. When they return to their team with the cotton ball, they must place it in the egg carton in one of the unoccupied spaces. The first team to fill their egg carton wins.

"Do-It-On-Paper" Shuffle

In this relay each person on a team receives two pieces of paper. (Newspaper works fine; keep plenty on hand.) The first players for the teams move between two points stepping only on the paper. They lay a piece of paper in front of themselves and step on it. Then they pick up the paper behind them that they just stepped off of and place that paper in front of them and step on it, and so on. If a player touches the floor, that player must return to the starting line and begin again. The object is for a player to race on the paper to a goal and return to her team. The first team whose players complete their trips to the goal and back wins.

Feet on the Rocks

Divide your group into two teams that sit back-to-back in chairs placed at three-foot intervals. The captain of each team sits in a separate chair at the front end of his team's row of chairs (see illustration).

At the signal an ice cube is placed under one of the feet of each captain. The captains slide the ice to the first player on their teams. That player must pass the ice cube from one foot to the other and then to the next player on the team. This continues until the ice cube is passed to the last player on the team and then back to the captain. The captain now devises a way to carry the ice cube (using feet only) to the opposite end of the room and put it into a cup. If the captain drops the ice cube, he can

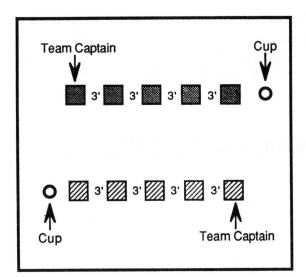

start from where it was dropped, but if the ice cube melts or slips out of reach while the team is passing it, they must start over again.

Gotcha Relay

Divide the group into two teams. Set up the room or field similar to the diagram. Each team lines up single file behind their respective markers. On "Go!" the first players begin running around the track (in one direction only) just like in a regular relay race. On completing the lap the runner tags the next player who takes off in a similar fashion. The team whose runner catches up and tags the opposing runner ("Gotcha!") wins.

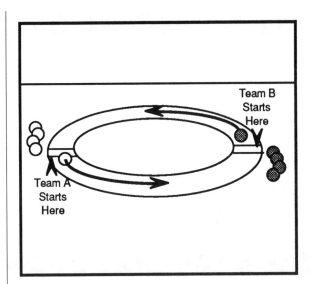

Hand-In-Glove Relay

This is a relay game in which the teams stand in line and race to be the first team to pass a pair of gloves from one end to the other. The first person puts the gloves on, then the next person takes them off of the first person and puts them on himself. Each person takes the gloves off the person in front of him and puts them on himself. All fingers of the hand must fit in the fingers of the gloves. Options: Use kitchen gloves or large work gloves.

Hovercraft Drag Races

Set out 8½-by-11-inch sheets of paper, crayons, pencils, and markers. Instruct your group to design their own sports car—a flat, two-dimensional dream machine, colored from a bird's-eye view. Encourage them to use their imaginations—to name their cars, cover them with sponsor's names and logos, and number them. Remind the group members to distinguish the front from the rear.

The drag strip is a table; provide start and finish lines. Owners of the hovercraft dragsters puff lightly on the rear of the vehicles to float them down the strip and across the finish line. Leaving the strip (falling off the table) and spin-outs (when the rear of the dragster is farther down the strip than its front) disqualify the "drivers." Drivers can race the clock or each other in time trials and tournaments.

The final race can be a Hovercraft 500. Set a square racetrack using four tables, divide your young people into teams (placing some puffers on the inside of the track), and let each team race the clock for the best time.

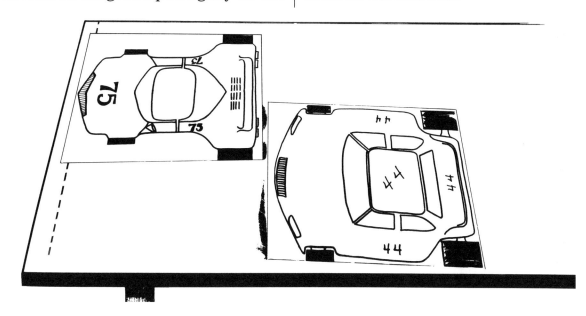

Hula Hoopla

The hula hoop will never die. It has been around for quite a few years and should be around quite a few more. Here are four hula-hoop relays that can be a lot of fun. Divide into teams and run these relays in normal relay fashion. Each team should have a hula hoop, which can be purchased at most toy stores.

1. Place a hula hoop on the floor twenty feet in front of each team. The object is for each player to run to the hoop, pick it up, and "hula" around five to ten times (your group can decide how many), drop the hoop to the floor, and

return to the line.

2. The object of this relay is for each person to take a hula hoop and hula while walking or running to a point twenty feet from the team and back. If the hula hoop drops, the player must stop, get the hoop going again, and continue.

3. Place the hoop twenty feet away from the team once again. This time the player must run to the hoop and try to pass it over his body without using his hands. In other words, he must stand in the hoop and work it up and over his head using just his feet, legs, arms, etc., but no hands.

4. This relay is similar to the one above except two or three people run to the hoop at the same time and, without hands, work the hoop up around their waists. They then run to a point and back with the hoop in place around their waists. At no time may their hands be used to hold the hoop up.

Human Obstacle Course

For this relay each team lines up single file. Ten additional team members (or adult workers) are the obstacles: a "pole" to circle around, leg tunnels to go under, kneelers-on-all-fours to leap over, sitters with outstretched legs to step in and among. On signal the first person in line goes completely around the pole, under the tunnels, over the kneelers, in and among the sitters (not missing any stepping space), around another pole, and then back to his team to tag the next runner. If an obstacle is missed or improperly executed, the runner must repeat that obstacle.

Leapfrog

This traditional relay race is still lots of fun. Two or more teams are formed with an equal number of players on each. All the teams are lined up behind the starting line. The first player on each team takes a standing broad jump as far as she can jump. That player then squats and bends over.

The next player runs and leaps over the back of the first player, propelling himself with both hands and pushing off the back of the first player as he leaps over. This second player squats and bends over where he landed, while the third player leaps over the first player, then the second player, and finally squats and bends over where she landed waiting for the fourth player to leap, and so on.

A player can begin leaping before the teammate in front of him has squatted. A player must leap over the back of each teammate in order and land on his own feet before leaping over the next teammate. Any player who can't leap over the back of a teammate or knocks over a squatting teammate must return to the starting line. The object of the game is to see both how far and how fast a team can move itself.

Light-As-A-Feather Relay

Break into as many teams as you like. Give each team a feather and a paper plate. Teams need to line up behind a starting line. On a signal the first player on each team takes off for a goal line carrying the paper plate with the feather in the middle of the plate. If the feather falls off the plate, a player can try to catch it on his plate and continue racing toward the goal line. If, however, the feather touches the ground, the player must return to the starting line and begin again. You can also use balloons instead of feathers.

Mad Relay

This is a different kind of relay race in which each player does something different. What the players do is determined by the directions in a bag at the other end of the relay course.

At the beginning of the relay, each team lines up single file as usual. At the signal the first person on each team runs to a chair at the other end of the course and pulls a slip of paper with instructions written on it from a bag sitting on the chair. The player reads the instructions and follows them as quickly as possible. Before returning to the team, the player must tag the chair. The player then runs back and tags the next runner. The relay proceeds in this manner. The team that uses all of its instructions first is the winner. Below are a few examples of directions:

1. Run around the chair five times while continuously yelling, "The British are coming, the British are coming!"

2. Run to the nearest person on another team and scratch her head.
3. Run to the nearest adult in the room and whisper, "You're no spring chicken."
4. Stand on one foot while holding your other foot in your hand. Tilt your head back and count down from ten to one and then shout, "Blast off!"
5. Take your shoes off, put them on the wrong feet, and then tag your nearest opponent.
6. Sit on the floor, cross your legs, and sing the following: "Mary had a little lamb, little lamb, little lamb, Mary had a little lamb, its fleece was white as snow."
7. Go to the last person on your team and make three different "funny-face" expressions, then return to tag the chair before tagging your next runner.
8. Put your hands over your eyes, snort like a pig five times, and meow like a cat five times.
9. Sit in the chair, fold your arms, and laugh as hard as you can for five seconds.
10. Run around the chair backwards five times while clapping your hands.

Message Relay

Each team divides in half and stands thirty to fifty feet apart. The leader stands in the center holding pieces of paper with crazy messages written on them. Write one message per team. At the signal one of the members of each team runs to the center, grabs a piece of paper, reads the message, wads it up,

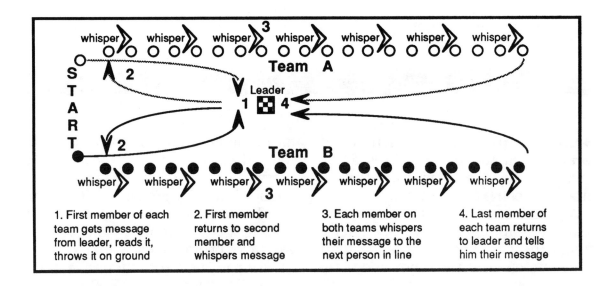

1. First member of each team gets message from leader, reads it, throws it on ground
2. First member returns to second member and whispers message
3. Each member on both teams whispers their message to the next person in line
4. Last member of each team returns to leader and tells him their message

and throws it on the ground. She then runs to the half of her team that is on the opposite side from which she came and whispers the message in the ear of the first person in that line. The one who hears the whispered message runs across to the other half of his team and whispers it to next person in that line. This continues until the last person runs to the leader in the center and tells the leader the message. The team whose final message is closest to the original message wins. Although the players must act quickly, accuracy in transmitting the message, not time, is most important. Sample message—"Ms. Sara Sahara sells extraordinary information to very enterprising executives."

Root-Beer Relay

Here's a good one for your next picnic or outdoor event. Get some cold root beer and some root beer mugs. Five players from one team sit on one side of a picnic table, and five from the other team take the opposite side of the table. Set a full mug of root beer in front of each player. When the whistle blows, the first person on each side starts drinking down his root beer. When a player finishes drinking the root beer, he sets his empty mug down on the table, and the person next to him starts drinking. Players continue down the line. Meanwhile, the ones who have finished are getting refills. When the last person is finished, start over again with the first person. It's that second time that makes this game really wild. The first team to finish the second round wins.

If you have lots of teams, do it tournament-style or race for times. It's a lot of fun to mix parents and young people together (but don't have parents and related kids on the same team). A variation is for the players to use straws. You can also rotate in other players to drink the refills.

Seat Scooters

Divide into teams of two. Create a winding race course with a start and a finish line. The course can be twenty to thirty feet in length. Couples sit on the floor facing each other with shoes together and holding hands. The couples alternately bend and straighten their legs to propel themselves around the course.

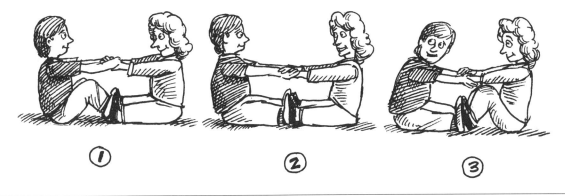

① ② ③

Spit-Wad Relay

Divide your group into teams. Have each team line up single file facing a prepared target about ten to twenty paces away. Each team member is given a plastic straw and told to guard it with his life. Each player also receives five small pieces of paper to be used as spit wads. The first player on each team is the shooter. At the sound of the whistle players begin chewing up the paper into little balls. One at a time, each person in line blows the spit wad through the straw at the target. They will usually stick to the target. After shooting one spit wad, each player goes to the end of the line. The next player shoots, and so on until all shots have been fired. Safety guards should stop players shooting other players, or you'll have a spit-wad war on your hands.

Tire Grand Prix

Lay out a course in a safe, open area, and give each player an old tire. Then have players race, rolling their tires around the course. Or you can make the race a team relay, stationing players every fifty yards along the course. At each "pit stop" the player passes the tire on to a fresh driver. For added fun allow players to kick, knock over, or in any way impede the progress of the opposing racers, while still trying to get their best time. Alert safety guards to watch for unnecessary roughness. Old tires can be borrowed from a cooperative tire dealer or service station.

Toilet-Paper Relay

Have each team line up single file with the first player holding a roll of toilet paper over her head. At the signal each team unwinds the roll down the line until it is gone. First team to use up the entire roll wins.

Weird Barrow Race

This is a variation of the old wheelbarrow race where Player A becomes the wheelbarrow by walking on her hands while Player B, using player A's feet as handles, simply runs along behind. In this game you do basically the same thing with the added difficulty that the wheelbarrow (Player A) must push a volleyball along the ground with her nose. This can be done as a relay by pairing team members and racing the pairs against each other.

CHAPTER 7

Fantastic Team Games

Children at this age love team competition. Stir in a healthy dose of unskilled competition, add a dash of cooperation, and watch them have fun!

Remember the leftover party balloons you would bounce around in the air when you were a child, trying to keep them from hitting the ground? What was rainy day entertainment then still works with young people today. Formalize the game a bit by making two teams that try to hit the balloon away from the opposition. Teams must alternate hits (only one hit per team), and are not allowed to hit the balloon directly at the floor. The two teams intermingle in a designated playing area. Scoring can run like this: intentional grounding scores a point for the opposition, as does two consecutive hits by members of the same team. If the balloon touches the ground, the point goes to the team that hit it last.

As a variation to intermingling the two teams, put teams on opposite sides of a six-foot-wide "dead zone" (volleyball fashion) and permit each team three hits (by different players) before returning the balloon across the dead zone. More than three hits per team or more than one hit per person scores a point for the opposition. If the balloon lands in the dead zone, the point is scored against the team that last hit it. A team serves until it loses a point.

Balloon Burst

Divide your group into two teams and pick a captain for each team. Arrange the teams as diagrammed below. Each team tries to hit the balloon in the direction of its captain, who then bursts the balloon with a pin. One point is scored for each balloon burst. Players must stay seated and use only one hand.

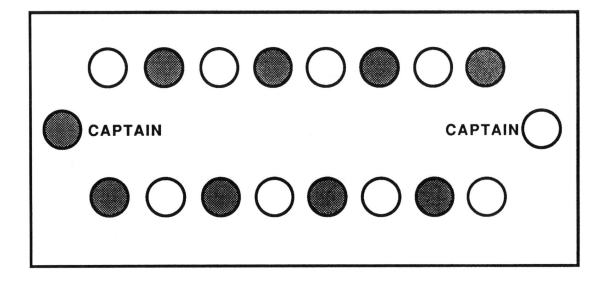

Battle for the Sahara

This is a game for two or more teams in a large outdoor setting. Each team has an empty water container and must transport water from a neutral or "safe" water source across the "Sahara" (a playing field 1000 to 2000 feet long) to their team's water container, which is also in a neutral or safe zone. The object is to fill their team's container before the other team can fill its own water container. The hazard is that on the playing field, players tagged by certain other players must empty their cups, return to the water source for a refill, and try again to transport their cupful of water across the Sahara.

Each team consists of one "general," one "bomb," three "colonels," four "majors," and five or six "privates." (For a smaller or greater number of players, adjust the number of majors, colonels, and privates on the team.) Each person carries a secret ID card marked with his rank. Each player (except the general) has a water cup, and each team has an empty gallon container in their own neutral zone.

Each player (except the general) travels to the water-supply area with her cup, fills it with water, and returns to her team's water container to pour her cup of water in it. While en route a player may be tagged by any opposing player who is carrying a cup full of water. Players with empty cups cannot tag. If a player is tagged by an opposing player of a lower rank, the lower-ranking player must empty his own cup. If a player is tagged by an opposing player of equal rank, neither player empties his cup—both continue their journeys. If a player is tagged by an opponent with a higher rank, the tagged player must empty her cup. After any tag both players must show their ID cards to determine who must empty the cup.

All ranks except the bomb may tag other players (although the private has no use for tagging, being the lowest rank.) The bomb carries water but may tag no one. Anyone tagging the bomb, however, is automatically demoted to private and must empty his own cup. Anyone demoted to private must give up his ID card to the bomb, who then turns it in to one of the safety guards at the earliest opportunity. (This keeps people in the game).

Any player who accidentally empties the cup of an opposing player must escort the offended player while she both refills her cup and pours it in her team's water container. The general doesn't have a cup and is free to tag other players at any time. A general can also run interference for lower ranking teammates carrying water. Station safety guards along the route to make sure no there's no foul play and that offended players get their free escorts properly.

Bedlam Elimination

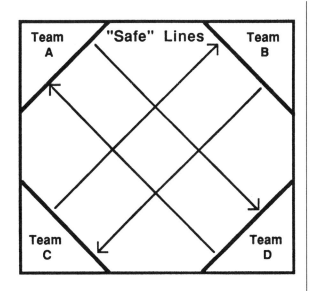

This game adds a new dimension to Bedlam (page 31). Divide your group into four equal teams. Each team gathers in a different corner of the playing area within the lines drawn on the floor designating that area as "safe."

Team members receive a flag like those used in flag football, which must hang free from the back of players' waists. (If you do not have access to ready-made flags, create your own by ripping old sheets into strips.) When a signal is given, team members attempt to get to the opposite corner of the room without losing their flags. As players pass through the middle of the playing area, they can grab one or more of the flags from players of the three other teams, as long as the player grabbing a flag still possesses his own flag. Once a player's flag is gone, so is that player. (For best results each team should wear a different-colored flag. This will prevent players from replacing their own missing flags with captured flags.)

After the first round each team is reduced in size because so many players lost their flags in the bedlam during the crossing of the play area. At a second signal these reduced teams try again to cross the play area diagonally to their safe zone. The games continues until only one member of one team is still wearing his flag.

To slow the action down for safer crossings and to add an extra dimension to the game, require the kids to move across the playing area in a variety of ways—on one foot, on their hands and knees, without shoes, etc. Safety *must* be stressed to players concerning teams crossing in the middle.

(Just for fun, see if you can say the title of this game ten times really fast without making a mistake.)

Bubble-Blow Blitz

Give each team a bottle of bubble solution and a bubble pipe. Have the team captain stand ten to twenty feet away from the goal line making bubbles while her teammates blow them across the goal line. The team that blows the most bubbles across the goal wins. (Switch team captains after each round so that all the team members get a chance at it.)

If you play this indoors, draw the goal line only ten feet away from the person blowing the bubbles. Dead air does not allow the bubbles to be blown more than a few feet. When playing outdoors the goal line can be fifteen to twenty feet away from the captain. (This game will not work on a windy day).

Contest of the Winds

Draw a large square on the floor similar to the diagram below. Divide the square into four equal parts designated as North, East, South, and West. Divide the group into four teams. Scatter dried leaves or cotton balls evenly in each quarter of the square. At a given signal the "winds begin to blow" and each team tries to blow (no hands allowed) the leaves out of their square into another. Set a time limit, and the team with the least leaves (or cotton balls) in their square wins.

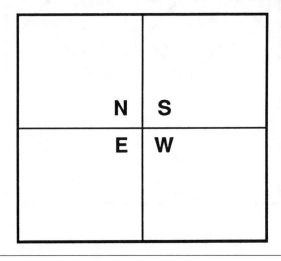

Dunce Bombers

Here's an indoor game that kids will scream for again and again. Two teams are chosen at random and seated on opposite sides of the room. Each team is given a supply of newspaper "ammo." Each team also has a dunce, who sits with a large cup balanced on his head somewhere near the back of the players. All players must stay seated in one spot on the floor throughout the game.

The object of the game is to knock the cup off the head of the other team's dunce with wadded newspaper. The dunce cannot use his hands in any way, but other team members can bat down flying paper bombs as long as their seats don't leave the floor. A point is scored each time a team knocks off the other team's dunce cap. Teams can use a variety of large and small bombs, paper airplanes, machine gun blasts, cooperative barrages, paper clubs, etc. to knock down bombs. The game usually takes a stack of newspaper two to four feet high.

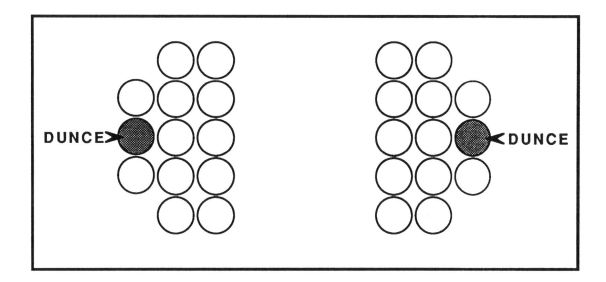

Feet Ball

This active indoor game requires real team work. Divide the group into two teams and seat them in two rows of chairs facing each other. The object is for each team to move the ball (a playground ball, plastic ball, or slightly deflated volleyball) through their goal by using their feet only. The goals are at the opposite ends of the line. Players must keep their arms behind the chairs to keep from incurring a penalty by touching the ball. To begin the game, drop the ball midway between the two goals in the middle of the two teams. The game can be any length desired. To avoid injuries to feet, kids must remove their

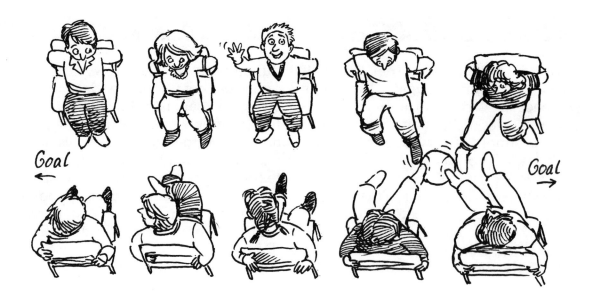

shoes. Also make sure the players on the teams are far enough apart that their feet barely touch when they extend their legs to the sides. The safety guards should guard against unnecessary roughness as well as keep the score even by dropping the ball back into play (when it is kicked out of play) at strategic locations between the teams.

Hudson Bay Versus Northwest Fur Trading Company

Play this game where there's plenty of running room, varying terrain, trees, and other good places to hide. Two teams are given adjacent territory and different-colored arm bands to distinguish them. Clearly mark the dividing line between territories. The object of the game is for each team to find "furs" in their own territory and deliver them to their team's headquarters (which happens to be located in the other team's territory). Thus, the fur traders must carry a load of furs (up to five each) across the boundary line separating the two teams, through enemy territory, to the safety of their post (a large circle). The furs can be up to 200 two-inch by six-inch strips of cardboard.

The Hudson Bay fur should be marked with an "H" and spread in one team's territory; the Northwest fur should be marked with an "N" and spread in the other team's territory.

Teams may search for furs in their own territory and then deliver them to their headquarters. They can also send their players into enemy territory to hunt for their opponent's furs, which they may attempt to deliver to their own headquarters. In other words, a team can take their opponent's furs if they are willing to risk hunting in enemy territory. Once they cross into enemy territory, carrying their own furs or hunting for their opponent's furs, they can be "killed" (tagged) by the other team, and whatever furs they are carrying are seized and taken to the tagging team's headquarters. All players tagged in enemy territory must also give up their arm bands to the tagging player, and no fur can be taken into headquarters by players missing their arm bands. Players who are killed return to their side of the line, pick up a new arm band from a safety guard, and start again.

Stop the game after twenty to thirty minutes. The team with the most furs in its headquarters wins. To encourage players to risk their lives to get enemy furs, a team is awarded double points for every enemy fur delivered to that team's headquarters (e.g., 100 points for every fur of their own delivered, 200 points for every enemy fur delivered). Have quite a few safety guards on duty throughout the entire game.

Human Lawn Mowers

In a park or in a big back yard, divide into teams and give each person a pair of blunt children's scissors. Each team has a container that team members attempt to fill with grass cut by the scissors. No pulling of the grass by hand is allowed. At the end of the time limit (five to ten minutes), the team with the most grass wins. Safety guards can penalize a team for infractions of the rules.

Indoor Murderball

Here's an indoor game for two teams of at least five players each (teams may be larger in larger rooms). In a large room that is nearly indestructible, line up two teams of equal size against opposite walls, about three feet from the wall. Team members then number off.

A light, plastic ball is placed in the middle of the room. The leader calls out a number, and the two players with that number (one from each team) run out to the middle and by throwing, kicking, or carrying the ball try to hit the opposite team's wall with the ball. The team standing in front of the wall tries to prevent the ball from hitting their wall. Whichever player doesn't have control of the ball attempts to block the move,

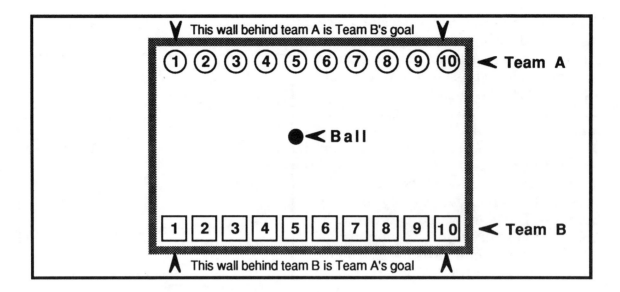

but she cannot touch the player with the ball or the ball itself as long as the other player holds the ball in his hands. That means the player without the ball can only block a shot. Once the ball hits the opposing team's wall or is blocked and caught by a member of the opposing team, the round ends. Put a time limit on each round of play. And keep your safety guards active.

Paper Route

This game is an adaptation of the Chariot Race game in which kids are pulled around a track on a blanket. In Paper Route the rider on the blanket is

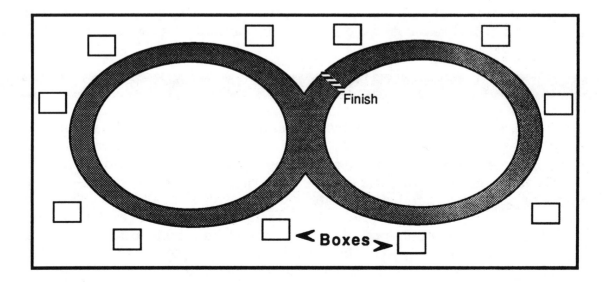

given an armload of "newspapers" to deliver as she is being pulled around the room. Cardboard boxes or trash cans can be used as houses along the way, and the papers must be tossed accurately into them for points. Each player gets the same number of newspapers; newspapers tossed unsuccessfully cannot be retrieved.

Another variation is to seat teammates in chairs along the route, but far enough away that the paper would have to be tossed a good distance. The person in the chair must catch the paper without leaving the chair. For added excitement have several teams going at once with their courses crisscrossing, going in opposite directions, and the like.

Warn the group to remember safety. They shouldn't pull the blanket so suddenly that a rider could fall back and hurt himself. Place safety guards strategically around the track to keep things from getting out of hand.

Paper Shoot

Divide into teams of four to eight players each. Set a three-foot-high garbage can in the middle of the room. Prepare ahead of time several paper batons and a lot of wadded-up paper balls. One team lies down on their backs around the trash can with their heads toward the can. Each of these players has a paper baton. The opposing team stands about ten feet away in a circle around the trash can. The standing team tries to throw their wadded-up paper balls into the can, and the defending team tries to knock the balls away with their paper batons while lying on their backs. The opposing team gets two minutes to shoot as much paper into the can as possible. When the time is up, count the number of wads in the trash can, then let the teams trade places and play again. The team that landed the most paper

balls into the can is declared the winner. To make the game a bit more difficult for the throwers, have them sit in chairs while they toss the paper.

Pop-Can Bowl

Divide your group into two teams positioned on opposite halves of a recreation room, gymnasium, or other playing area, and supply players with several playground balls. Between the two teams is a three-foot-wide "can zone," where dozens of empty pop cans stand. Players must bowl the balls into the cans in order to knock them into the other team's playing area without crossing into the "can zone" themselves. The team with the least cans in its area after two minutes of playing wins. Play as many rounds as you like.

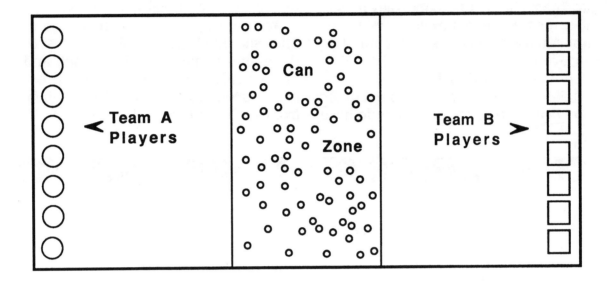

Q-Tip War

Divide your group into two teams separated by a line down the middle of the room, give each player five to ten Q-Tips and a straw, and open fire. The object is for each team to blow-gun as many Q-Tips across the line onto the enemy's side of the room as possible before time runs out—purposely firing on opposing team members is not allowed). Players can reload with Q-Tips shot over onto their side. After time is called, safety guards count the Q-Tips on each side. The team with fewer Q-Tips on their side wins.

River Raid

Play this game outside the church building by dividing into two teams and arming them with rubber bands and five to ten paper bullets, as illustrated below. Each team begins at opposite ends of the church. The object of the game is for the two teams to exchange positions—but they must follow the same trail to get there. On the way they can eliminate opposing team members by shooting them on the legs or below with their paper bullets. The team who completes the exchange with the most surviving players wins. Players who are shot must go to a neutral zone until the game is completed.

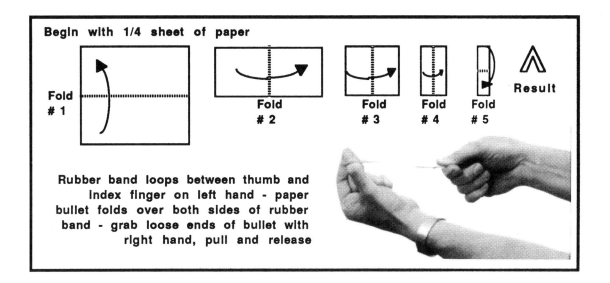

Begin with 1/4 sheet of paper

Fold #1 Fold #2 Fold #3 Fold #4 Fold #5 Result

Rubber band loops between thumb and index finger on left hand - paper bullet folds over both sides of rubber band - grab loose ends of bullet with right hand, pull and release

Or you can also play a variation where players that are shot join the other team as captured prisoners. In this variation any captured player must give up his ammo (paper bullets) to the person who shot him and must stay with that person as a prisoner. If, however, the prisoner is tagged by one of his teammates, he is freed. The freed prisoner will have his gun but no ammo since it was relinquished. He will have to share paper bullets with teammates or go without.

You can add to the excitement of the game by having more than one route. There will be lots of skulking, some huge shoot-out scenes, and strategies for penetration and avoidance, offense and defense.

Make sure kids don't shoot each other in the face. Keep several safety guards on patrol throughout the game. Although these rubber-band paper-shooters are reasonably safe, there is a slight chance of getting shot in the eye. Therefore, recommend that all players wear sunglasses while playing.

Shock

This is a good game for large groups. Two teams containing the same number of players hold hands in a single-file line facing each other. At one end of lines on the floor or a table, there is one spoon. At the opposite end of the lines are two players, one from each team, with a coin.

The two people with the coins begin flipping them (like a coin toss) and show-ing the coins to the first person in line on their teams. If the coin is "tails," nothing happens. If the coin is "heads," the first person quickly squeezes the hand of the second person, who squeezes the hand of the third person, and so on down the line. As soon as the last person in line has received the squeeze, that player grabs the spoon, sets it back on the floor or table, and runs to the front of his team's line to take the place of the coin flipper. Everybody else moves down one place. This continues until every player has been the coin flipper and the spoon grabber. The first team to get its original coin flipper and spoon grabber back into their original positions is the winner.

No one may squeeze the next person's hand until their own hand has been squeezed first. This is like an electric shock that works its way down the line. A safety guard should be stationed at both ends of the team lines to make sure everything is done legally. A false shock results in a one-place penalty for that team and a new coin flip. You might want to have everyone practice their squeeze before starting so that everyone knows to squeeze good and hard. Otherwise they might confuse a little twitch for a legal squeeze.

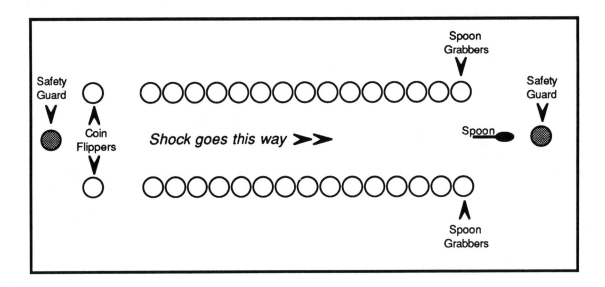

Snow Blow

For this game all you need is a big bag of Styrofoam packing chips. Mark out an X on the floor, divide your kids into four teams, assign each team to one of the quadrants in the X, and pile a small mountain of packing chips in the outside corner of each quadrant. At the whistle each team, on hands and knees, tries to blow all their chips into neighboring quadrants while keeping all other chips out of their own quadrant. All usually goes well until borderline clashes occur—and then what a mess!

Space-Ball Countdown

Here is a fast, exciting, and rough game that requires teamwork—and kids love it. Form two equal teams with one team forming an evenly-spaced rectangle or circle and the other team inside the circle as dispersed as possible. When the whistle sounds, the team outside tries to hit every member inside as quickly as possible with one, two, or more Nerf or other soft balls. When a player is hit, she or he must fall to the ground and lie still. Head hits and bounce hits are illegal.

When everyone has been hit, the clock stops, the time is recorded, and the teams change places. The team with the shortest time in the outside circle wins. You can score the best two out of three rounds or combine total times. Be sure to have players remove glasses and aim shoulder level and below. If you wish to make the game more challenging, have the outside group take one or two steps back after each round, giving the inside circle players more room to roam.

Target Practice

On a table set against a wall, place twenty to forty targets made from papers folded in half. These targets vary from two inches to about six inches in size. Put point values on each one (10, 25, 50, 100) depending on the size of the target. Each team gets an arsenal of rubber bands. All players stand behind a line fifteen feet away and hit as many targets as possible in one minute. The team with the most points wins.

Terrible Twos

Here is a fast, competitive game that can be organized in just a few minutes using ordinary household items. Go around the house and locate about thirty or forty pairs of things (two shoes, two hammers, two bookends, two records, two bars of soap, two toothbrushes, etc.). Add several items which have no mate. Put all this stuff into a big box and mix it up thoroughly. Then divide your group into two teams standing an equal distance away from the box. (If this game is played indoors, place the pile of stuff in a separate room.)

On "Go!" each team sends a player to the box and she brings one item back to the team's "stockpile." Each successive team member does the same thing in turn, taking care not to bring back an item that has already been brought back by a teammate. The players race through their lineup as many times as possible within a set time limit, bringing back as many items as they can.

If a person brings back an item that is already in the team's stockpile, it must be spotted by the team and sent back with the next runner, who may not bring back a new item on that turn. If the item is not spotted right away as a duplicate item but is left in the team's stockpile, it will count against them when points are added up at the end of the game. When the whistle blows (this should occur before the entire stock of items is exhausted), points for each team are awarded as follows:

1. Each item is worth ten points (total of items times ten).
2. Each item with no mate is worth fifty more points.
3. Each pair of objects stockpiled by the same team is worth a *minus* fifty points per item (100 total minus-points per pair).

For experienced players make each team's stockpile a large box where items are deposited out of sight. Kids must memorize each item as it goes in, increasing the likelihood of ending the game with more duplicate items in the box. Another way to add difficulty to the game is to create pairs of items not identical to each other, but still creating a "pair." For example, you might have a toothbrush and toothpaste, a hammer and a nail, a cup and saucer, etc.

Tug-O-War Times Two

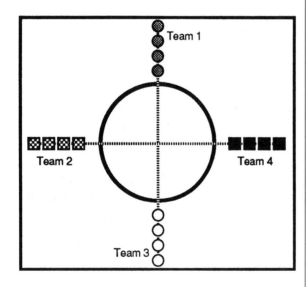

By tying two ropes in the middle so that you have four ends of equal length, you can have a tug-of-war with four teams instead of two. Draw a circle on the ground so that each team is outside the circle when the war begins. When one team is pulled across the circle line, it is eliminated from the game, leaving the other three teams to tug against each other. Those three play until another is eliminated, and finally two teams play to determine the winner. Each time the tug-of-war is conducted across the circle.

For a tug-o-war times three, tie three ropes in the middle and make six teams compete. It works! The primary advantage to this version of tug of war is that the weaker teams can gang up on the stronger teams and equalize the competition.

Wacky Sports Events 1

If your group loves traditional sports but you are concerned that the competition is out of hand, try these traditional sporting events with a twist.

This crazy variation of baseball works best with large groups. Turn a two-foot-high wastebasket upside down to be the crock, which is home plate, and place first base thirty to forty feet away from home plate. (Shorten or lengthen this distance as needed.) There are no other bases. The playing field is 360 degrees around home base; there are no foul areas.

Fielders can stand anywhere except close to home plate. Place the pitcher's mound about twenty feet from home. The team at bat lines up to one side of the crock. Batters may use any type of a bat and must hit a large playground ball or slightly deflated volleyball. The pitch must be lobbed up over the crock in an underhand manner, and the batter may wait for a pitch that is in the strike zone. If the pitcher knocks over the crock, then a run is scored for the team that is at bat. An umpire to call balls and strikes is not necessary because any time the batter swings the ball is in play—even if he misses the ball.

Once a player hits the ball, she must run to first base and back to the crock to score a run. The opposing players chase the batted ball and throw it to the pitcher, who must knock over the crock with it before the runner returns, thus making it an out. (The pitcher should change every inning, so that one person does not dominate the game.) If the batter hits a long ball, she may choose to run from home to first several times to score several runs all by herself. The only way to get the batter out is to knock over the crock after the ball is in play. You can call caught fly balls out if you want, but it's more fun to have every ball (hit, not hit, caught, not caught) knock the crock over for an out.

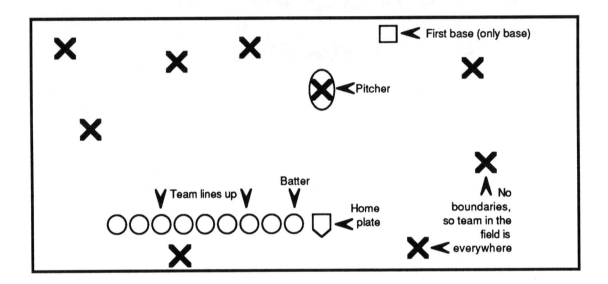

Fat Bat

Here's a version of baseball that can be played outside in any kind of weather. Purchase a Fat Bat and Fat Ball from a toy store or department store. They are easy to find and inexpensive. Regular baseball rules apply, only there are no foul balls. Everything is fair. Players don't use gloves, either. The ball is so light that a good wind will carry it all over the place. So, the nastier the weather, the better.

Fuzzy Ball

Here's an indoor take-off on baseball perfect for groups of ten to fifty. You'll need a "fuzzy ball"—one of those softball-size nursery toys with a rubber center and fabric covering—and a plastic Whiffle-Ball bat. (In a pinch you can use a Nerf or foam ball and a broom.) Lay out home plate and three bases, divide players into two teams, and play ball— well, play Fuzzy Ball. Here are the differences from normal baseball:

• With a hit, players run first to what is

normally third base, then to what is normally first base, then to what is normally second base, then home.

- Runners are put out only by a tag or by throwing the ball and hitting them below the shoulders. Catching fly balls and tagging bases are not outs.
- Everyone on a team gets to bat only once each inning regardless of how many outs they have. (Outs retire runners from base running; they don't determine the length of the inning.)
- The team at bat supplies its own pitcher; a maximum of five pitches are allowed to each batter.

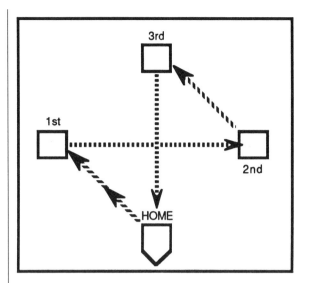

Nerf Baseball

For this indoor activity all you need is a Nerf baseball (3½ inches in diameter), a Whiffle bat, and a room large enough to place eighteen-inch square masking tape bases fifteen to twenty-five feet apart. The pitcher's mound is about fifteen feet from home plate. Rules are the same as regular baseball except the runner can be put out if she is not on a base and is hit by the Nerf ball; there are no force outs—the runner must be tagged; and the pitcher is supplied by the team at bat.

Ping-Pong Baseball

Here's a good baseball game that you can play indoors. All you need are ping-pong balls and a ping-pong paddle for the bat. It requires a lot of room and is very fast-moving and exciting to play. If the ball hits the roof on a fly, it is playable, but the walls are foul territory. All the usual rules of baseball apply, or your group can create their own rules.

Ping-Pong-Home-Run Derby

You can play this all-or-nothing version of baseball with just a handful of kids, a fair-sized room, a ping-pong ball, and a paddle for a bat. Set four or five folding tables on their sides as a playing field fence (see diagram). Use masking tape to form a home plate and two foul lines. Now for the rules:

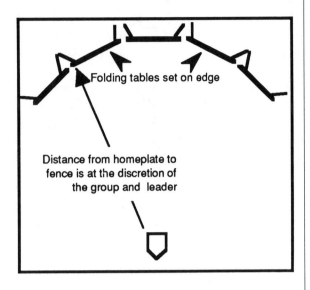

Folding tables set on edge

Distance from homeplate to fence is at the discretion of the group and leader

- All players must play on their knees.
- There are no strikes, no balls, no base hits—just home runs or outs.
- A player gets a home run when the ball he hits clears the fence without touching the floor or ceiling. If a hit ball touches the floor or ceiling or is caught or swatted down by a fielder, the batter is out. Foul balls are played over.
- The fielding team, which plays along the inside of the fence, tries to swat a hit ping-pong ball down before it flies over the fence.
- Each team gets three outs; play as many innings as you like. The pitcher can be a sponsor who pitches to both teams or a member of the team at bat. You may choose to have an umpire/ scorekeeper.

Score Ball

This variation of baseball is a great equalizer; non-athletic types do as well as your group's jocks. All you need is an indoor or outdoor playing area marked into zones (as diagrammed below), a bat, and three different-colored Nerf or foam balls.

Divide into two teams. The fielding

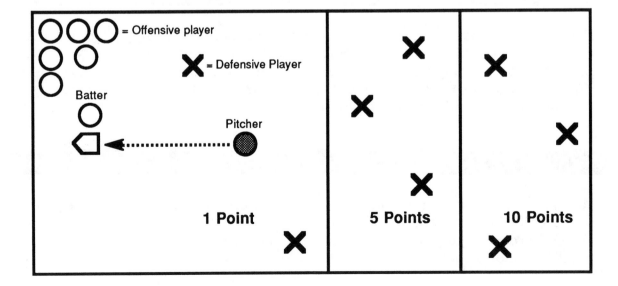

○○○ = Offensive player

✗ = Defensive Player

Batter

Pitcher

1 Point   5 Points   10 Points

team spreads out in the field, while the team at bat sends its first member to the plate to hit. A batter receives only three pitches; three strikes puts her out, as does a caught fly ball. The three colored balls are pitched in the same sequence for each batter. Here's why: the first pitch (e.g., the red ball) is worth one point if it's hit; the second (yellow), two points; the third (blue), three points. Colored balls make it easy to keep track of the points. So a batter may choose either to hit whichever ball comes her way or to wait for the second or third pitch for more points.

There's more—the point value of a hit ball is multiplied by the point value of the zone it lands in. For example, if a player hits the second pitch (two points) into the middle zone (five points), she earns ten points for her team. A hit, therefore, can earn anywhere from one to thirty points. The pitcher is supplied by the team at bat.

Sock Ball

This version of baseball can be played indoors with regular baseball or softball rules or Crockball rules (page 91). The twist? Everything is made out of socks. Stuff a large sock full of smaller socks to make a sock bat. You can make a sock ball the same way. No shoes are allowed during the game. This game can really be a riot.

Nerfketball

Here is a fun version of basketball using a Nerf ball and chairs. Choose two teams of equal numbers and seat them alternately on sturdy chairs as shown in the diagram—two rows of players facing each other. For best results space players at least double arm's distance apart both sideways and across. Place a "basket" (small bucket, gallon plastic bottle with the top cut off, wastebasket, etc.) on the floor at each end of the double row, approximately six feet from the players at the ends of the rows.

The two ground rules of the game are:
• Chairs cannot be moved or tipped.
• Each player must remain seated while the ball is in play.

Using a coin flip, one team is chosen to take first possession of the ball. The team tries to work the ball toward their goal by passing it, while opponents try to block passes and steal the ball. Any player may take a shot at the goal at any time, but the advantages of passing the ball to the player nearest the goal are obvious. If the ball is intercepted by the other team, play continues in the opposite direction.

When an attempted field goal misses, the ball is automatically "out" to the other team, and play then goes the other way. When a field goal is scored, all players rotate one seat to the right. This will give each player the opportunity to be her team's prime shooter during the game. After rotation the ball goes "out"

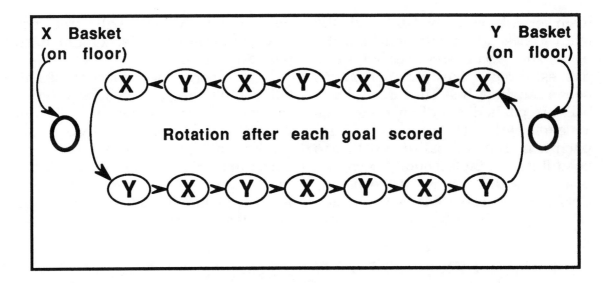

to the other team, and play goes the other way.

Any ball loose within the playing area is a free ball. Any ball going outside the playing area is given to the player nearest the last player to touch the ball.

Penalties may be assessed and free throws awarded for players leaving their seats or engaging in unnecessary roughness. Use a kitchen timer for quarters or halves, or set a scoring limit.

Ping-Pong Basketball

In this team competition players bounce ping-pong balls into different size containers. Vary the amounts of points given depending upon difficulty—the smaller the container, the larger the amount of points given. The balls must bounce at least once before going into a basket. This makes for great team competition.

Refrigerator Ball

Here's a good game for your next outdoor meeting pushed inside by bad weather. You need a large room, a standard refrigerator (or something similar), a light playing ball, and a cardboard box. Weight the box and place it on top of the refrigerator, which is placed in the center of the room. Draw a circle on the floor around the refrigerator so that players can't get closer than four feet or so. Then let them play regular basketball. The team that has the ball may pass it around and then take shots at the "basket," trying to get the ball to stay in the box. The excitement is increased by missed shots going over the box to the opposing team, shots being "tipped," etc. Make up your own rules as you go along. A safety guard can call fouls and keep things from getting out of hand.

Ring-Net Ball

Here's a basketball/baseball-type game perfect for a gym night. As in baseball the defense scatters themselves around the basketball court. From the sideline at mid-court, an offensive "batter" throws a basketball in the "field" (the court). She then runs out to the "base" (the circle at mid-court) and runs around it as many times as possible before the defense can grab the ball and sink a basket. Score one point for each completed circle around the base, as judged by a safety guard. Everyone on the team throws before the inning switches.

Capture the Football

Adapted from Capture the Flag (page 32), this game can be played by smaller groups with less room, and it doesn't have to be completely dark. Instead of using flags, use footballs placed in each team's territory. A team must get the opposing team's football over to their team's territory. To accomplish this a team may pass or run the ball over the line to win. If any player is tagged, he must remain a prisoner of the opposing team until a teammate tags him. If a player passes the football to a teammate over the line and the teammate drops it, both players become prisoners. If the pass is complete, that team wins. Adapt Capture the Flag rules to your group and setting for the best results.

Feather Football

Choose two teams, and everyone gets down on their hands and knees. Goal lines are marked on each end of the room. A feather is placed between the two teams, and the idea is to blow the feather across the opposing team's goal line. Limit this game to about six persons to a team.

Human Football

This wild game can be played on any rectangular playing field, outdoors or indoors. A normal football field works fine. There are two teams with any number of boys or girls on each team.

When a team is on offense, they begin

play at the twenty-yard line. They get four downs to move the ball down the field and score a touchdown. There are no additional first downs. Here's how yardage is made for the offensive team: a player hikes the ball to a quarterback, who is then picked up in a sitting position and carried by the rest of the team down the field. The entire team must be joined together, either carrying the quarterback or by holding on to the team members carrying the quarterback. Your safety guards can monitor this for safety.

The defensive team begins each play lined up on the goal line that they are defending. As soon as the offensive team hikes the ball, the defensive team locks arms and moves down the field toward the offensive team, now on the move towards them. When the defensive team reaches the offensive team, the two end members of the defense try to dislodge one of the offensive players from the rest of their team (only the *end* members are eligible to dislodge the offense, because only they have a free arm each to grapple; all other defensive players' arms are interlocked).

All teams must walk while the ball is in play. If the defense breaks its chain, they must reunite before proceeding down the field.

If the offensive chain breaks, the down is automatically over. The ball is then put into play from that point. The defensive team returns to the goal line on each play, and the offensive team repeats the same procedure. If no touchdown is scored in four tries, the defense becomes the offense and gets the ball at the twenty-yard line going the other direction. Score the game any way you wish.

Circle Soccer

Two teams stand in a circle, half on one side and half on the other.

Throw a playground ball or partially deflated soccer ball into the circle for the players to kick out through the other team's side. If the ball is kicked out over the heads of the players, the point goes to the non-kicking team. If the ball is kicked out below the heads of the players, the kicking team gets the point. Hands may not be used at all to deflect the ball, only feet and bodies. No one may move out of position except one pre-selected player per team, who may kick the ball to her teammates if the ball gets stuck in the center. The player who can move may not score, however, or cross into the other team's territory. If the roaming player gets hit with the ball (when kicked by the other team), the kicking team gets a point.

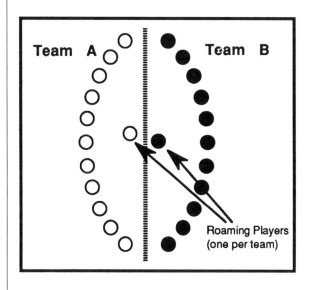

Four-Team Soccer

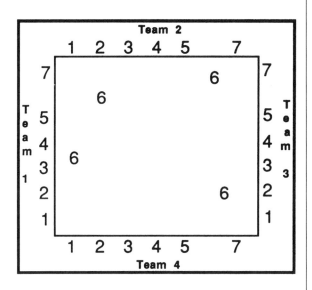

On a large, square playing field with clearly marked sidelines, position four equal teams (as diagrammed below) who try to score goals by kicking a soccer ball through any one of the four sidelines. Each team's players distribute

themselves evenly along their sideline, and each team member receives a different number, starting with one and numbering consecutively.

Each round begins when one of the safety guards calls out one or several numbers. The players who have those numbers run to the ball in the middle and attempt to kick the ball over one of the other team's sidelines. Soccer rules are used to advance or stop the ball. Play continues until a team scores.

If no team scores within a few minutes, call another number to bring in new players or stop the play and call in a completely new set of numbers. A score is made when the ball is kicked through any team's line. The ball must be shoulder height or lower to counts as a goal. Team members protecting the sidelines *can* use their hands to block or catch the ball. The ball is returned to play by a two-handed overhead toss.

Have one of the safety guards keep track of which numbers have been called so that each number is called an equal number of times. Safety guards should periodically announce the scores so teams can then gang up on the leading team. The game will stay amazingly close.

Line Soccer

If you want a simple, indoor/outdoor variation of soccer, this game is for you. Divide your group into two equal teams that line up opposite each other about thirty feet apart on two sides of a playing area. Each team numbers off successively. Draw a line in front of each team to designate the scoring area.

A ball is placed in the middle of the field, and a referee calls out a number. The players on each team with that number run out to the ball and try to kick it across the line guarded by the opposite team. The ball must pass between players below the head (or the waist, if you prefer) in order to count as a goal. It may not go over their heads. The defenders can catch the ball and toss or kick it back to their own player when it comes to them. After a minute or two, a safety guard calls out a new number. It really gets wild when you call out several numbers at once.

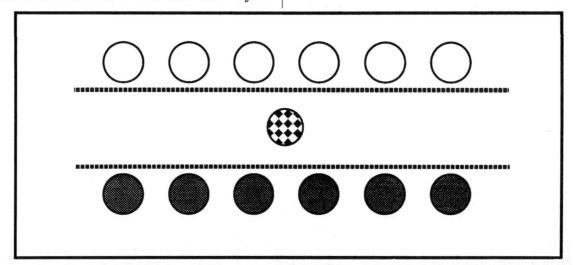

Soccer on Paper

In this indoor game players (including the goalies) must play soccer while standing on a piece of newspaper that must remain in a marked spot for the entire game—no scooting. The rules are like regular soccer, but players must keep one foot on their papers at all times. Be sure to scatter players on both teams evenly all over the playing area. Once the players are settled on their papers, toss in a soccer ball and watch the fun. The effect is like a giant pinball game.

Wacky Sports Events 2

More favorite sporting events with a twist.

Paper Badminton

For this indoor variation of badminton use a racquet made of a sheet of ordinary 8½-by-11-inch sheets of paper. (Old church bulletins work fine.) Fold the sheet in half and staple it along two edges. The thicker the paper, the stronger the racquet. Each player's hand goes inside the paper like a glove.

For the net use a string with strips of newspaper hanging from it. You can use a stapler to attach the paper. A wad of paper makes the "birdie." Play by whatever rules you wish.

Bottle Bowling

Use plastic milk bottles, thirty-two-ounce soda bottles, or half-gallon milk cartons for pins and a volley ball for a bowling ball. Set the pins twenty to twenty-five feet away from the bowler and bowl away. This is a great game for picnics and a breather during all-day game events.

Tire Bowling

Just about any service station or tire store will gladly give you some old tire casings in a variety of sizes. The tires take the place of bowling balls and kids are used as pins.

Divide the group in half; one team bowls, the other acts as the pins. The people pins are set up just like regular bowling pins, only spaced about two to three feet from each other. The pins are allowed to lean away from the tire as it comes at them, but they must keep both feet together unmoved. If they move either foot at all, the bowler gets the pin.

(Mark the spot where the pins should stand with a piece of masking tape.) Let one team bowl, then switch places.

The trick to hitting as many as possible is to roll the tire wobbly and try to get it to fall down in the midst of the people pins, striking several as it falls. As the people pins are touched, they move out of the bowling lane. Caution: Tire casings are dirty, so wear grubbies and have wash-up facilities handy. (If you have a small group, use cans, milk bottles, or plastic soda bottles for pins.)

Anti Dodge Ball

Children love this new twist on dodge ball. Two teams play in a square playing field, a gym, or a parking lot. Establish a center dividing line and have teams take their sides.

Teams score by rolling or bouncing the playground ball across the opposing team's outer boundary line while trying to block the other team's attempts to do the same. The ball *must* be rolled or bounced. (This eliminates potential injury by strong-armed throwers.) The game an be played by points or by time. Safety guards also act as point judges.

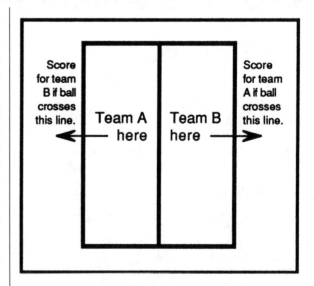

Four-Team Dodge Ball

This fast-moving game best played in a gym or similar room requires four teams of equal size. If you have a basketball court marked on the floor, this can be used as the playing area; otherwise you will need to mark off your own boundaries with tape or some other method. The floor is divided into quadrants like the diagram below:

Each team is assigned one of the four areas, and team members cannot leave their assigned area during the game unless they are hit with a thrown ball. Use a playground ball or beach ball to play a regular game of dodge ball, except a player may throw the ball at anyone in any of the other three quadrants. If a player is hit below the belt with the ball, that player becomes a member of the team that hit her and must move to the throwing team's quadrant. If the ball misses and goes out-of-bounds, a safety guard tosses the ball to the team that was thrown at. If a player throws a

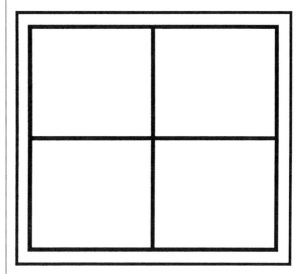

ball and before it bounces another player catches it without dropping it, the player who threw the ball becomes a member of the team that caught the ball. The winning team is the team with the most players at the end of a specified time period.

Water-Balloon Dodge

This game is exactly like dodge ball, except you use water balloons. You can also use water baggees (see page 63). Line one team up against the wall and the other team a minimum of twenty feet back. Instead of a player being eliminated when hit, he becomes a member of the team throwing the water balloons.

Balloon Golf

Great for playing in a small room, this game can also be played outdoors when there is no wind. First, drop a penny or smooth rock into a round balloon. Then blow the balloon up to about a five-inch diameter. Make golf clubs by rolling a full sheet of newspaper into a stick. Cardboard boxes are used as the holes with the par for each hole written on the side of the box. (Don't make par too low. You may want to shoot the course ahead of time to establish the par.) The weight inside the balloon creates a kind of Mexican jumping bean effect, causing both difficulty and hilarity for all the players.

Kick Golf

No green fees for this round of golf. Set up your own nine-hole course: Hula Hoops are the "greens," small sticks stuck within them are the "flags," and small playground balls are the "golf balls." Players can kick or roll the ball with their hands, so there is no need for golf clubs. Roll the ball up against the stick and consider it a hole.

For each hole lay a marker to show where players tee-off. And don't forget to set par. Use hills and other obstacles—traps—to vary the difficulty of each hole. Distribute score cards, and play by teams.

Broom Hockey

This game can be played with as many as thirty or as few as five per team, but only five or six players from each team are on the field at one time. For a team with thirty members, for example, have them number off by sixes, giving you six teams of five members each. Let all the 1s play a three-minute period, then the 2s, etc. Two teams compete by running out onto the field at the signal, grabbing their brooms, and swatting through the opposite goal a volleyball placed in the center. Each team has a goalie who can grab the ball with her hands and throw it back out onto the playing field. If the ball goes out-of-bounds, safety guards throw it back into play. Player cannot touch the ball with hands or kick it; they may only hit it with the broom. Score one point for each time the ball passes between goal markers.

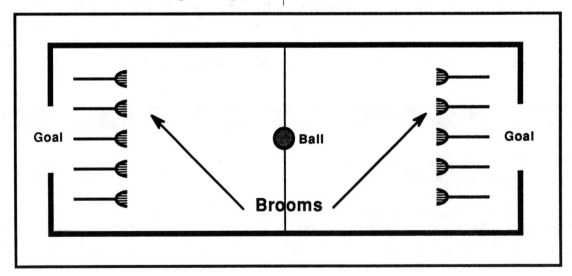

Expandable Hopscotch

If your kids like Hopscotch, they should love Expandable Hopscotch. Secure small carpet remnants from any carpet store. These are then used as hopscotch squares. The game is played as usual, except that the squares are spaced further and further apart as the game progresses until the kids are jumping several feet between squares. It's great fun and great for laughs.

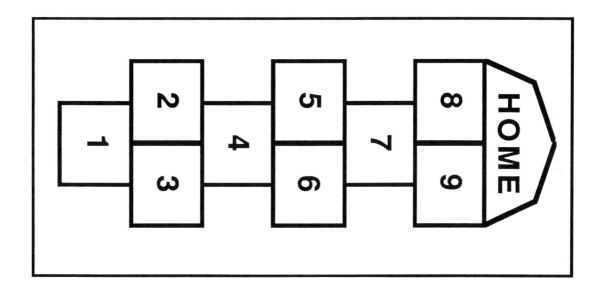

In case you've forgotten how to play hopscotch, here's a quickie refresher course. Draw out on a sidewalk a chalk diagram with nine squares and a semicircle as home (see diagram).

Players decide who will go first, second, third, etc. The first player begins by tossing a small rock (or other small object) into square one. The player then hops over square one and places her left foot in square two and her right foot in square three. She hops through the remaining squares on one foot in the single squares and one foot in each square of the double squares. When she reaches home, she turns around on one foot and hops back through the squares to number two and three, where she stops to pick up her rock before hopping into square one and out of the hopscotch.

The first player repeats the process, except she throws the rock into square two, then three, and so on. A player's turn is over when she steps on a line, misses a throw, loses her balance, hops in a square containing the rock, or does not correctly pick up the rock. Players begin where they left off in their next turn at play.

The object of the game is for a player to successfully toss her rock "home" after hopping through all the previous squares according to the rules.

Balloon Pong

All set up for ping pong only to find no one brought ping-pong balls? Get some balloons and play this slo-mo version of ping pong. Line your kids up in two lines, one against each end of the ping-pong table. Players play according to regular ping-pong rules, except that they hit a balloon (weighted with a marble inside) instead of a ball. The real catch is that there is only one paddle between the two teams.

After a player hits the balloon, he slides the paddle under the net to the opposing player, who grabs the paddle and returns the balloon ping-pong fashion. After a player makes his shot and slides the paddle to the other player, he scoots out of the way to the back of his line as quickly as possible. Players may keep the balloon aloft with their breath if they need time to snatch the paddle.

Ping-Pong Ball in the Cup

Here's a game for a large room with a cement or tiled floor (to provide plenty of bounce). It's both fun to play and to watch. The only props you need are ordinary ping-pong balls and plastic drinking cups. Break the group into pairs. With ten to twenty feet between partners, one player throws the ball to her partner, who must catch the ball in the cup either on the fly or on the bounce. A catcher cannot use her hands and must catch the ball before it stops bouncing. The catchers become pitchers by returning the ball after retrieving it from the cup (or floor). Any time the ball stops bouncing before it is retrieved, the pair gets a point. At the end of a period of play, the pair with the fewest points wins.

Water Pong

For this fun variation of ping pong, fill two small saucers or shallow bowls full of water and place them about twelve inches from the net on either side of center line. Using regular playing rules, players try to put the ball into the opposing player's saucer to win the round. The game is scored normally, but ends if the ball lands in a player's saucer.

Slow-Gear Games

Slow your group down a bit with these less active yet still fun games.

Artists' Imagination

Divide into teams that have a pencil and several pieces of paper. One member of each team is sent to the middle of the room. The leader whispers the name of the item that the players must draw upon returning to their groups. On a signal each representative returns to her team and without talking or voicing any sound begins drawing. The artist cannot write any words on his drawing. Team members try to guess what the artist is drawing. The first team to shout out the answer wins. Items to sketch could include:

a pizza

a paper clip
a Sunday school teacher
a mirror
a tube of toothpaste
a telephone
a banana split
the three bears

A variation is to have the group draw pictures representing biblical stories such as:
the Flood
the second coming of Christ
the woman at the well
the last supper
Daniel in the lion's den

the good Samaritan
Jonah and the whale
David and Goliath

Cain and Abel
the Sermon on the Mount

Bite the Bag

Stand a grocery bag in the middle of the floor and ask everyone to sit in a wide circle around it. One at a time each person must come to the bag and try to pick it up with just his teeth, then return to a standing position. Nothing but the bottoms of a player's feet are ever allowed to touch the floor. Almost everyone can do this. After everyone has a turn, cut off or fold down an inch or two of the bag. Go

around again. With each round shorten the bag further. When a person is no longer able to pick up the bag and stand again, she is out. The winner is the one who can pick it up without falling when no one else can. For safety's sake, especially as the bag gets lower to the ground, you will want to place an adult leader or two on the sides or in front as spotters.

Cootie

Here's a fast-moving game that your kids will want to play over and over again. All you need to play is pencils or pens for all players, a supply of Cootie Score Sheets (on the next page), and a die for every five players. Break into groups with no more than five players per group. Each group needs a stack of score sheets, a die, and pencils or pens for every player. Each groups rolls the dies to see which player starts. The player with the highest roll plays first.

The object of the game is to draw the body of the Cootie (as shown on the score sheet) by rolling the appropriate numbers on the die. A cootie has thirteen parts, each represented by a number on the die as shown below:

1 - Head   4 - Ears
2 - Body   5 - Tail
3 - Eyes   6 - Legs

In order to draw a complete Cootie a player would have to roll one 1 (head), one 2 (body), two 3s (eyes), two 4s (ears), one 5 (tail), and six 6s (legs). But there is a catch—a 2 must be rolled (to draw the body) before any other rolled numbers can be used.

Each person takes a turn rolling the die as rapidly as possible. Once a player throws a two, she can draw a Cootie body on her score sheet. A player continues to roll the die and draw a cootie as long as she rolls numbers that can be used. Once a player rolls a number she cannot use, the next player rolls. That player must also roll a two to begin drawing. The score sheets have space available for ten rounds of the game.

COOTIE SCORE SHEET

	# On Die # On Die 1 - Head 4 - Ears 2 - Body 5 - Tail 3 - Eyes 6 - Legs	**Round 1**
Round 2	**Round 3**	**Round 4**
Round 5	**Round 6**	**Round 7**
Round 8	**Round 9**	**Round 10**

Geiger Counter

Seat everyone in the room and select one player to be "It." "It" leaves the room. While "It" is away, the group agrees on a hiding place for a random object (someone's comb, a wallet, a book), which the leader hides. "It" returns and tries to find the object not knowing what it is. The rest of the group makes ticking noises much like a Geiger counter. As "It" moves away from the object the group ticks slower. As "It" moves closer to the object, the group ticks faster until "It" finds the object.

A variation of the game is to select an object already in the room for "It" to identify.

Gum Sculpture

Everyone is given equal amounts of gum to chew. Then they are given a 4 x 6 note card and a toothpick. They must sculpt their gum using their toothpicks. Players can make anything they want within a given time. Judge the sculptures and make everyone a winner. Have categories for ugliest, most creative, weirdest, etc.

I Spy

Similar to Geiger Counter (see above), this simple game has been played for years. One player is chosen to be "It." He chooses an object in the room and says, "I spy with my little eye something that begins with the letter . . . ," and names the letter (if "It" chose the wall clock he would say the letter "c"). Group members can now ask questions of "It" to help them identify the object. "It" can answer only "Yes" or "No." The first player to correctly guess the object becomes the new "It."

Killer

In a group of less than forty people, everyone sits in a circle (in chairs or on the floor) and faces inward. The leader has a deck of playing cards, and he lets everyone in the room take one card without showing it to anyone. (There are only as many cards in the deck as there are people in the room.) One of the cards is a "Joker," and whoever draws it becomes the "killer." No one, of course, knows who the killer is except the killer himself. Play begins by everyone looking around at each other and talking casually. The killer "kills" people by winking at them. When a person is winked at (killed) that player waits five seconds and then says, "I'm dead," or falls over dead. The object is to guess who the killer is before being killed.

Once someone is winked at, she is

dead and cannot reveal to the group who winked. Anyone making a wrong guess is also dead. If someone is asked if he is the killer, that person must answer truthfully. The killer tries to see how many people he can pick off before getting caught. When the killer is caught, the cards are collected and shuffled, and the game is repeated for as many rounds as there is time. If you do not wish to use playing cards, use note cards or slips of paper. Place a large dot on one of the papers indicating to the person receiving it that he is the killer.

Out of Step

Players form a circle. "It" performs a motion that everyone can see and mimic (scratching his head, rubbing his belly, jumping up and down). After doing the motion twice, "It" performs another motion and another and another. Once "It" starts performing the second motion, the group of players mimics the first. When "It" completes the third motion, the players perform the second. The players should always be one motion behind "It." This pattern of play continues until a member of the group makes a mistake. At this point the person sitting to the right of "It" becomes the new "It."

Rhythm

Everyone forms a circle and counts off consecutively from one to however many kids are in the circle. Player number one begins the rhythmic pattern of first slapping thighs, then clapping hands, then snapping right hand fingers, then snapping left-hand fingers. The motions should be done at a moderately slow speed in a rhythmic fashion. (It may speed up after everyone learns how to play.) Once the rhythm is established, the whole circle joins in performing the rhythmic pattern.

The real action begins when the number one calls out his own number on the first snap of the fingers and then calls out somebody else's number on the following snap. For example, it might sound something like this: slap, clap, "One, six!" In this example number six must then choose another number during the slap and clap so that when he snaps he can say his own number on one snap and another player's number on the second snap—slap, clap, "Six, ten!" Then number ten would do the same thing.

If anyone doesn't call the numbers rhythmically on the snaps, or if a player calls the number of the player who just called him, that player goes to the end of the numbered progression, and everybody who was after him moves up one number. The object is to eventually arrive at the number-one chair.

Silent Act

Choose two teams to play this game which is similar to Charades. Team A leaves the room to choose a word that Team B will have to guess. Team A must also think of a hint word that rhymes with the chosen word. For example, if the group decides upon the word "sock," their hint word might be "rock."

Team A returns to the room and one team member repeats aloud the hint word for Team B. No other speaking can occur. Team B must now guess the word and communicate their guess to Team A by acting it out. For example, after hearing the word "rock," Team B, which can only communicate among itself by gestures, might decide to act out the word "lock" by miming locking a door. Or they might act out the word "sock" by acting like they are untying a shoe, removing the sock, and waving it about for Team A to see. Only five team guesses are allowed, which encourages the groups to work together in determining their group guess. If a group guess is incorrect, the other group shakes their head no and says, "Aaaah." Once a team correctly guesses the word or else uses up all five of its guesses unsuccessfully, the two teams switch roles and play resumes.

Wipe That Smile

Players are seated in a circle. The leader smiles then wipes the smile off his face by wiping his hand across his mouth. The leader, no longer smiling, takes the smile in his hand, walks to another player, and hands that person the smile. That player must put the smile on with her hand by placing her hand over her mouth and then smiling. That player wears the smile for a few seconds before taking it off and giving it to a new player. No one in the circle can smile at any time except for the player wearing the smile. The object of the game is to catch players smiling out of turn. Anyone caught goes into the middle of the circle and is allowed to smile, make faces, etc. to get the players still in the circle to smile out of turn.